THE ETERNAL WOMAN

Gertrud von le Fort

THE ETERNAL WOMAN

The Timeless Meaning of the Feminine

Translated by
Marie Cecilia Buehrle

Foreword to the New Edition
by Alice von Hildebrand

IGNATIUS PRESS   SAN FRANCISCO

Cover art: *Virgin Annunciate*, Batoni Pompeo (1708–1787)
Réunion des Musées Nationaux / Art Resource, N.Y.

Cover design by Riz Boncan Marsella

© 2010 by Ignatius Press, San Francisco
All rights reserved
ISBN 978-1-58617-298-5
Library of Congress Control Number: 2008933485
Printed in the United States of America ∞

CONTENTS

Foreword to the New Edition

There are books that being timeless are always timely. This is why the reprinting of Gertrud von le Fort's *The Eternal Woman* should be not only welcomed, but acclaimed.

The felicitous title of this great book is taken from the famous words of J. W. Goethe: "Das Ewig-weibliche zieht uns hinan." (The eternal feminine draws us on.) They refer to woman's role in time because her meaning hints at eternity. With unfailing female intuition, von le Fort addressed this topic of crucial and perennial importance: the role of woman in the salvation of the world, which is the battlefield between good and evil, life and death.

Since the Garden of Eden, the Evil One and the Woman have been in the arena. And the weapon chosen by man's enemy today is once again a seemingly innocuous question: "Why are women humiliated and looked down upon by the Church?" Indeed, why? Are not questions legitimate?

Yes, but there are questions that are raised *only* when a person has adopted a wrong metaphysical posture. This, in turn, leads him to put God in the dock and arrogantly challenge him to justify his decisions. Among such questions: Why should women deliver their children in pain and anguish while for men procreation is nothing but a moment of ecstasy? Is not maternity an obstacle to a woman's development, locking her in the narrowness of her home and condemning her to petty, mediocre work for the sake of husband and children? Why should women, usually more intuitive than men, be refused the dignity of the priesthood?

Forgotten are the privileges granted to woman from the very beginning: her body is not taken from the dust of the earth but from the flesh of a human person; she is exalted by being called "the mother of life"; she is the one whose reproductive organs are "veiled"—and the veil not only symbolizes the sacredness of her task as life bearer, but also hints at the fact that a female womb would, one blessed day, be a tabernacle inhabited by the Holy One, the savior of the world, who would have a human mother but no earthly father.

In 1934, when *The Eternal Woman* was published, the poisonous blossoms of feminism were still in the bud. But Gertrud von le Fort, endowed with a prophetic sense, refuted the spurious claim that the metaphysical equality of man and woman means their identity. This conclusion leads to the horror of "unisex," in which the sexes are not complementary but interchangeable. This is debasing for both men and women. As noted by G. K. Chesterton, a contemporary of von le Fort: "There is nothing so certain to lead to inequality as identity" ("Woman and the Philosophers").

In contrast, *The Eternal Woman* exalts the feminine. How profoundly does von le Fort show the superiority of the sacred over the secular, of *genitum* over *factum*, of maternity over productivity, of mission over profession. She outlines admirably the mystery of femininity: "The unveiling of woman always means the breakdown of her mystery", and the mission of woman is primarily a religious one. A highly cultivated woman, she wove her insights with artistic and literary references that are so enriching because they are not the fruits of abstraction but of meditation upon personal, lived experiences.

Such fruitfulness is also evident in von le Fort's other works such as *The Song at the Scaffold* and particularly in her sublime *Hymns to the Church*—a literary *Te Deum* for her conversion. The latter work so impressed my late husband, Dietrich von Hildebrand, that he had it printed by the Theatiner Verlag, the Catholic publishing house he had founded in Munich a few years before.

This event established a close contact between the two authors who shared many common interests, including a love of cats. Von le Fort was a pedigree cat breeder and when she discovered that von Hildebrand and his first wife were also fond of these graceful felines—whose main raison d'etre is to delight men by their beauty—she gave them a superb angora that was given the name of Ildefons. This enchanting animal had a privileged life but was lonesome, so von le Fort gave him an equally lovely companion named Suleika. They lived in perfect monogamy (not being permitted to leave the house), and gave much joy to the von Hildebrands.

This very Franciscan love of God's creatures inevitably led von Le Fort to a feeling of awe for the dignity of *human* life. With female intuition, she seemed to anticipate the gravity of our contemporary situation, foreseeing the coming war on maternity as a crime whose horror threatened the future of humanity and is in fact a satanic attack on Mary, the blessed one who gave birth to the Savior who is *the way, the truth, and the Life.*

The author never loses sight of the outcome of this war between Life and Death. Throughout she is inspired by Mary, the great and joyful discovery that von le Fort, like other prominent Protestant converts, made upon entering the Church. The blessed one among women is Virgin, Bride, Spouse, and Mother; she is the Woman clothed with the sun, who will crush the head of the serpent. It is Mary who teaches that receptivity—total openness to God's word—is the royal road to holiness. When offered to become the Mother of the Savior, her response was fear, amazement, awe. But upon being promised that her virginity would be preserved, she spoke the blessed words that were going to open the door to salvation; "*Fiat*", "Be it *done* to me".

This gem of a book is a sublime meditation on the words of St. Paul: "For when I am weak, then I am strong" (2 Cor 12:10). It is when we acknowledge our helplessness that God's power is made manifest in us. *The Eternal Woman* is a clarion call to women: to imitate Mary, the Mother par excellence, is the road to victory: "I can do all things in him who strengthens me" (Phil 4:13).

—Alice von Hildebrand

FOREWORD TO THE 1954 EDITION

This book was first published in Germany, in 1934. At this writing, over one hundred thousand copies have been sold, and the original has so far been translated into French, Italian, Spanish, Portuguese, and Dutch. All these translations were difficult to provide, for the German version itself is not easy reading, and translating it in each instance constituted a task requiring unusual skill.

Various attempts were made in the English language. Excerpts of the book first became available to American readers in the New York *Commonweal*, in 1936. Now, at last, comes this full English translation which represents the best efforts of both translator and publisher to produce a classic in its own right.

It can be said without fear of contradiction that no book like this has ever before been written, none certainly on this difficult subject as penetrating and with as deep an insight. It is a book on woman written by a woman whose competence in dealing with her topic is unique. For Gertrud von le Fort not only is a trained philosopher and historian. She is also a highly gifted poet and, above all, steeped in the noblest traditions of the Christian past, which in the light of the present day she interprets with a rare mastery.*

Her biography is brief. Born on October 11, 1876, at Minden, Westphalia, she hails from a family of French origin.

---

* This foreword was written in 1954, before Gertrud von le Fort's death on November 1, 1971.—ED.

xi

Her forebears in France first immigrated to Italy in the sixteenth century and then settled in Geneva, Switzerland, but later generations moved on to Russia and eventually to Germany. Baroness von le Fort could not have wished for an education more enlightening than the history of her own family, which reflects nearly every facet of Europe's cultural and religious heritage.

Surrounded by a typically Protestant atmosphere, she spent a happy youth on her family's estate of Boek on Lake Mueritz in Mecklenburg. Her father, Baron Lothar von le Fort, was an officer of the Prussian army, carrying on, as it were, from where his ancestors in France had left off when they served in the armies of Louis XVI. Her mother, Elsbeth, likewise was of aristocratic lineage, née von Wedel-Parlow. In a small volume incorporating some of her memoirs Gertrud von le Fort has written of her parents with deep affection. After a happy and carefree childhood she enjoyed a private education at home and then attended a Hildesheim girls' college. After her graduation she enrolled at Heidelberg university.

At Heidelberg, and at the universities of Berlin and Marburg, she dedicated herself for several years to both historical and philosophical studies that, combined with travel, especially in Italy, helped her gain an appreciation of things Catholic. After the death of her parents she moved to Baierbrunn near Munich in the company of one of her sisters, and in 1926 she became a convert to the Catholic Faith. She was received into the fold of the Church universal in Santa Maria dell' Anima, the German parish church of Rome. Since the end of World War II she resides at Oberstdorf in the Bavarian Alps. Now nearly an octogenarian, but still of youthful temperament and vigorous in spirit, she continues to be actively engaged in her writing. Recently she was awarded the Annette von Droste prize of literature and the Munich poetry prize in Germany, and the Gottfried Keller citation of Switzerland. She is also a member of the Academy of the Gallery of Living Catholic Authors, of Webster Groves, Mo.

Gertrud von le Fort was first attracted to the Catholic Church as a young girl while visiting in the Rhineland. These impressions were deepened during her stay at the Hildesheim college, but did not really mature until she had the opportunity of a protracted residence in the Eternal City. Her superb first novel, *The Veil of Veronica* (which Sheed and Ward published in an English translation), reflects her Roman experiences. Eventually they led to her conversion. Her truly magnificent *Hymns to the Church*, beautifully translated into English by Margaret Chanler (another Sheed and Ward publication), had heralded this decisive event of her life.

Since then Gertrud von le Fort has been a prolific writer who soon gained prominence not only in Germany, but throughout Europe. Besides the two books mentioned, only her masterful novels *The Song at the Scaffold* and *The Pope from the Ghetto* are available in English.[1] Some twenty additional volumes, most of them poetry and novels, await translation. It is fervently to be hoped that these writings some day will all become accessible to the English-speaking world. They are on a level with those of the greatest Catholic and non-Catholic writers of this age and often reach the excellence of classics that will endure.

Gertrud von le Fort's message is drawn from the mainspring of Christian revelation. Her basic theme is that strength which

---

[1] *Hymns to the Church*, trans. Margaret Chanler (New York: Sheed and Ward, 1953), is an exception.—ED.

according to St. Paul "is made perfect in weakness" (2 Cor 12:9). Strength in weakness, in a power-drunk, secularized world bristling with arms and at the same time bleeding from a million wounds, because man, both physically and mentally, has run amuck!

In *The Song at the Scaffold*, Blanche de la Force, a young Carmelite novice, is portrayed as holding the likeness of the Christ Child in her arms. "So small and so weak", she says. But Sister Marie of the Incarnation replies: "No, so small and so powerful." Even more cogently Sister Marie adds a little later that "to tremble is to be strong", for in trembling we realize, as does fearful little Blanche, the very moment she is trampled to death by an infuriated crowd of revolutionists, "the infinite frailty of our vaunted powers".

In *The Wedding of Magdeburg*, a historical novel dealing with an episode in the Thirty Years' War, Gertrud von le Fort, in a breathtaking sentence, has thrown down the gauntlet to all the believers in a merely material progress, to all the worldly perfectionists and superficial rationalists. "Christ", she says, "does not emerge in a struggle *against* the Cross, but *on* the Cross—just as love always is triumphant in surrender." And this leitmotif keeps recurring throughout her writings to make us realize the paradoxy of Christian truth by the standards of eternal life. Seeming defeat ending in conquest, supreme sacrifice in triumph, Crucifixion in Resurrection—against the backdrop of historic scenes this appears as the fruit of all human experience, if we but tremble in the strength of Christ.

Perhaps the realization that man's weakness is his real and only strength, his surrender to God's holy will the only true victory he can achieve, perhaps such an awareness is more connate to feminine than to masculine nature. Of course,

we must understand these terms properly as spiritual principles and polar forces which can find their expression in
both man and woman. In both there can be pride, and
both can be children of Mary as true handmaids of the
Lord. It is from this premise that Gertrud von le Fort has
developed her profound metaphysical interpretation of womanhood. The eternal femininity as a theological mystery is
the subject matter of *The Eternal Woman*, which in her own
words deals with "the religious significance of femininity
and its ultimate reflection in God".

Again we must remember what St. Paul says about strength
being made perfect in weakness or, as some translators render the passage more aptly, power revealing itself in infirmity. Power and strength ultimately are not of this world,
but of the Kingdom of God. There is only one way to
achieve it: by surrendering to God's will. To use Gertrud
von le Fort's own words: "Surrender to God is the only
absolute power with which the creature is endowed." And
again: "To bring about his salvation, all man has to contribute is his readiness to give himself up completely. The
receptive, passive attitude of the feminine principle appears
as the decisive, the positive element in the Christian order
of grace. The Marian dogma, brought down to a simple
formula, means the cooperation of the creature in the salvation of the world."

Mary's fiat, then, her willingness to let God's will be done,
appears as the power in her infirmity. In woman's consti-
tutive desire to surrender, to give herself, rests the very depth
of life, for such surrender is the expression of the creature's
unquestioning acceptance of the will of God. That is why
Gertrud von le Fort says pointedly that "the world can be
moved by the strength of man, but it can be blessed in the
real sense of the word, only in the sign of woman."

In her novel *The Child's Kingdom*, which represents the introduction to a medieval trilogy not yet completed, Gertrud von le Fort has clearly indicated the sequence she has in mind. "First", she says, "comes creation which is the glory of God, then comes conception which is the humility of woman, and only then comes action which is the power of man." The implication is obvious that there can be no action, no "masculine" activity in life, without the "conception" of divine grace preceding it. Gertrud von le Fort throws further light on her reasoning when she goes on to say that "the hour preceding all creation is not called our power, but our helplessness—which is the only omnipotence." Helplessness thus is transfigured into "omnipotence", for by surrendering the creature becomes co-powerful with the Creator. All the achievements of man depend on this primary act of creative surrender, which leads to a divine partnership. Did not Christ himself tell Pilate that he would have no power unless it were given him from above? (Jn 19:11).

The issue is fundamental and should be brought home to all those who are willing to meet the challenge of Christian thinking. What Gertrud von le Fort says as a Catholic, others have expressed just as convincingly from their denominational perspectives: C. S. Lewis, for instance, when he wrote that "our role must always be that of patient to agent, female to male, mirror to light, echo to voice" (*The Problem of Pain* [New York: Macmillan, 1944] p. 39). The Anglican scholar proceeds to explain that our highest activity must be response, not initiative, because "our freedom is only a freedom to better or worse response." Nicholas Berdyaev, the late Russian philosopher, has reached conclusions along similar lines. "Within the sphere of humanity and in the natural world," he writes "there had to be a pure and spotless being capable of receiving the divine element, a feminine principle enlightened by grace" (*Freedom and the Spirit* [New York: Scribner's, 1935], p. 177). As one of the Greek Orthodox faith he sees this being in Mary, the Mother of God. Her fiat was "the answering love of man to the infinite divine love".

Modern man finds it difficult to absorb such thoughts, for he has torn off the veil of faith. He tries to deny the mystery of life and to ignore its transcendent reality. Woman is as much lost in the resultant chaos and anarchy as man. She has given up her birthright, as it were, by discarding the veil, by forcing her way from the depth of life to the foreground of life. In this light we can well understand how the symbol of the veil became a pivotal element in Gertrud von le Fort's thinking. It is an eminently feminine symbol that indicates that woman is inaccessible in her innermost being when she becomes the mother of life, and birth is born out of her depth, in silence and solitude. "The unveiling of woman", says Gertrud von le Fort, "always means the breakdown of her mystery." And she quotes the words of another great contemporary poet of Germany, Ruth Schaumann: "It is always the mystery which bears fruit while what is patent, and revealed, is an end."

On woman, then, centers the dominant issue of human history. Pride or surrender is the tremendous alternative. Clearly the struggle is not only one of our day, for the present is but a mirror of the past. There is an almost straight line linking up the naturalistic and pragmatist philosophies, which have weakened man's metaphysical outlook on life. The "age of reason" has led to an age of chaos. The schools of thought that made all values relative, or strictly secular and profane, developed of necessity an anarchic individualism that became the forerunner of modern paganism. Because it had become spiritually hollow and indifferent, the modern world apostatized morally and intellectually. Amid carnivals of despair man set up new idols, built new Towers of Babel, only to find himself lost in the mad whirl of demonic forces that nowadays has assumed gigantic proportions.

Amid this pitched battle between darkness and light it is woman's specific calling to restore the right balance that is a prerequisite of all stability. "Women", said Archbishop Richard J. Cushing of Boston, "must restore to political and professional life the emphasis on the spiritual, an emphasis now so sadly lacking; we rely on them to help win the spiritual battle against the evils of secularism." Dare we hope that in an age that cheapens womanhood by primitive and inanely vulgar displays, such higher ideals will prevail? Has the trend that started from the pretense that woman could make her best contribution toward human progress by being "equal" to man, rather than being herself, run its course? If woman, both physically and spiritually, fails to exercise her specific function as mother of life, mankind faces a vacuum where her mystery ought to bear fruit. In the midst of anarchy and despair the right balance must be restored between the masculine and the feminine forces, and woman must assert her influence as a woman, by means of her healing, womanly power, to restore order to a derelict human race. This book is an invaluable contribution toward that end.

MAX JORDAN
Beuron, Benedictine Archabbey
Marian Year, 1954

THE ETERNAL WOMAN

INTRODUCTION

This book is an attempt to interpret the significance of
woman, not according to her psychological or biological,
her historical or social position, but under her symbolic
aspect. This will imply a certain difficulty for the reader.
The language of symbols, once universally understood as
an expression of living thought, has largely given place today
to the language of abstract thinking; in consequence this
book must assume the obligation of clarifying for the reader
the character of the symbol.

Symbols are signs or images through which ultimate metaphysical realities and modes of being are apprehended, not
in an abstract manner but by way of a likeness. Symbols are
therefore the language of an invisible reality becoming artic-
ulate in the realm of the visible. This concept of the symbol springs from the conviction that in all beings and things
there is an intelligent order that, through these very beings
and things, reveals itself as a divine order by means of the
language of its symbols.

The individual carrier, therefore, has an obligation toward
his symbols, which remain above and beyond him, inviolate and inviolable, even when he no longer recognizes their
meaning, or when he has gone so far as to reject or deny
them. As a result, the symbol does not disclose the empiric
character or condition of the one who for the time being is
its bearer; but it expresses his metaphysical significance. The
bearer may fall away from his symbol, but the symbol itself
remains.

Just as the meaning of the symbol does not necessarily coincide with the empiric character or condition of the individual who for the time being is its bearer, so also the essential quality that it designates is not restricted to the individual in question. We maintain, for instance, that from the point of view of her symbol, woman has a special affiliation with the religious sphere. To conclude from this that woman herself is particularly religious, or that she holds supremacy over man in this respect, would imply a complete misunderstanding of this book. The matter concerns itself with the figurative aspect of the religious quality, its visual representation; and this, as belonging to the symbol, has been in a special measure entrusted to woman.

What is true of womanhood in its fundamental significance applies also to the meaning of its individual expressions. This book pertains throughout to revelation as it comes through woman; but she must never usurp the place of that which is revealed, insofar as its metaphysical reality is concerned; for here on earth the revelation of all being is a twofold one. This is precisely what the two forms of masculine life that are greatest in symbolic significance demonstrate. Thus in the really heroic manifestation of manhood the strong strain of womanly compassion appears, but under a masculine aspect: to the chivalrous man belongs the protection of the weak and helpless. Thus a St. Vincent de Paul, man and priest, takes the abandoned child of the stranger to his heart as a woman would. And thus in St. Aloysius Gonzaga, as well as in all typical figures of spiritual knighthood, virginity appears as also a masculine virtue.

It is a recognition of this twofold manifestation but from its other aspect, when St. Catherine of Siena regards precisely the virile virtues as essential to the truly Christian life, and the supreme acknowledgment of this duality, in accord with defined dogma, is included in the Litany of Loreto, which invokes Mary both as Mother most amiable and Virgin most powerful, and places the womanly image of Mystical Rose beside the manly symbols: Mirror of Justice and Tower of David. Like every truth concerning woman, this image of the Eternal Woman awakens also an understanding of the symbolic significance of womanliness. Mary, standing for the creature in its totality, represents at the same time both man and woman.

THE ETERNAL WOMAN

Wheresoever the created being enters into the concept of the eternal, it is no longer the creature that is expressed but the eternity of God, who alone is eternal. Only an age profoundly bewildered or misled in its metaphysical instincts could attribute the idea of eternity, be it regarded as absolute value or absolute duration, to a creature, without becoming aware that the latter, instead of being exalted, is thereby instantly annihilated. In its concept of eternity the created being acknowledges its own relativity and only in this avowal does eternity disclose itself to the creature.

The created being with its temporal limitations, its contingency, becomes submerged in the presence of the timeless, the absolute; and thus absorbed it appears no longer as a value in itself, but as a thought or mirror of the eternal, as its symbol or vessel. This is the meaning of all purification, of every religious surrender; it is the meaning of saint and lover; it is the meaning of death. This is the only sense in which we may here venture to speak of the Eternal Woman. Therefore it is by no means a question of presenting or even of transposing certain characteristics of the empiric image of woman that are relatively unchanging and might, in a restricted, earthly sense, be termed eternal. It is rather a matter of the cosmic, the metaphysical countenance of woman—of womanliness as a mystery, its religious rank, its archetype, and its ultimate image in God.

This implies obviously that every arbitrary and personal attempt at interpretation must be rejected. The religious, as we have seen, begins where the self-willed, the subjective, ends. But beyond this point what language shall we speak? We cannot grasp the metaphysical except under the veil of form, hence necessarily in the place where we find ourselves confined again to the lower level of the temporal and the relative. It is only great art in its supreme moments of inspiration that is capable of proclaiming under a transitory form the things that are unchanging.

As soon as we interrogate art, however, we are confronted by another revelation, namely, that our great occidental art can never be detached from Catholic dogma, that, under its supratemporal aspects, it is in fact its deputy priestess. Just as Beethoven's mighty *Missa Solemnis* continues to attract to the Credo of the Church thousands upon thousands whom the Church herself can no longer reach, so also great painting and sculpture carry throughout the centuries, even down to the modern pagan, the incontestable message of the Christian drama of redemption. An inquiry into occidental art not only in its aesthetic but also in its religious content means, therefore, to tread the ground of great Catholic dogma, the suprapersonal and supratemporal foundation upon which rests the total culture of the Western world, and to which, even in denying it, this culture is indissolubly bound.

Here first of all we must establish the fact that Catholic dogma has pronounced the most powerful declarations ever made about woman. In the face of these, all other attempts at metaphysical interpretation of womanhood vanish like a mere echo of theology, or as something meaningless so far as the religious sense is concerned. Not only has the Church in its teaching about the sacrament of matrimony compared woman, that is, every woman, to herself, but she has proclaimed a woman as Queen of Heaven; she has called her Mother of the Redeemer and Mother of Divine Grace.

By these expressions, it must be clearly understood, the Church obviously does not mean to imply the incarnation of womanliness in itself. She refers only to her who has been called "blessed among women". This blessed one, although she is immeasurably more than the symbol of womanhood, is nevertheless also this very symbol; for, in her alone, the metaphysical mystery of woman has assumed a form and hence become intelligible.

Here we shall try briefly to enlighten ourselves as to the content of the dogma. If we seek counsel from the great masters who depicted the life of Mary, Fra Angelico, for example, we must begin with his latest painting, for in reality it is the first. With intimations of that which is to come, religious art of the past reflects here, in the order of paintings, the later unfolding of Catholic dogma. Only in the last picture, that of the Coronation of the Blessed Virgin, does the Immaculata become entirely visible. This dogma, historically considered, has been defined late; metaphysically, however, it stands at the beginning of the mystery, even at the beginning of all things, disappearing as it were into the morning glow of the first hour of creation.

The dogma of the Immaculate Conception means the revelation of the human being when still unfallen; it betokens the undesecrated countenance of the creature, the image of God in man. From this point of vantage an extraordinary light falls upon the time when the dogma was defined. According to the Church in her concept of time, it came immediately before the moment that the

Christian historian and philosopher Berdyaev[1] character-
izes as that of the downfall of the human image, an association which only today we can recognize in its full
significance.

Here the tremendous and universal meaning of the Marian dogma already becomes clear. If the Immaculata is God's
inviolate image of humanity, the Virgin of the Annunciation is its representative. In the humble fiat of her answer
to the angel lies the mystery of redemption insofar as it
depends upon the creature. For his redemption, man has
nothing to contribute to God other than the readiness of
unconditional surrender. The passive acceptance inherent
in woman, which ancient philosophy regarded as purely negative, appears in the Christian order of grace as the posi-
tively decisive factor. The Marian dogma, reduced to a brief
formula, denotes the doctrine of the cooperation of the
creature in the work of redemption.

The fiat of the Virgin is therefore the revelation of the
religious quality in its essence. Since, as an act of surrender,
it is at the same time an expression of essential womanliness, the latter becomes the manifestation of the religious
concept fundamental to the human being. Mary is therefore not only the object of religious veneration, but she
herself is the religious quality by which honor is given to
God; she is the power of surrender that is in the cosmos in
the form of the bridal woman. It is this that the Litany of
Loreto means when, with the power of great poetry as well
as great dogma, it invokes Mary as the Morning Star. The
morning star rises in advance of the sun in order to lose

[1] Nicholas Berdyaev (1874–1948) was a prominent Russian historian and
philosopher. His books *The Meaning of History* and *The End of Our Time* are
probably the best known of his many writings. He was a firm believer in
Christianity and an adherent to its Russian Orthodox pattern.

itself therein, and the divine Son at Mary's breast signifies, with regard to her, that within the radiance of the Child she herself is submerged. Only in this sense is she the Mother of Divine Grace. In this capacity alone, she is also the Mother of the Cross and of Sorrows. As the glory of her Son outshines her, so his death struggle overshadows her. In her sorrow she is not only herself, but the surrendering one, the one who is suffering with her Son. But the compassionate one is likewise the co-redeeming one. This word, so frequently misunderstood, basically means only the mother: Mother of the Redeemer, Mother of the Redemption.

From this point the position of Mary in the history of Christianity becomes understandable. Seldom mentioned by the Evangelists, overlooked through long intervals in the history of the Church, Mary's great dogmas invariably arise at moments of gravest danger to the Christian faith. The fundamental dogma concerning her was proclaimed at the Council of Ephesus and constitutes a part of the refutation of the Nestorian heresy in its bearings upon Christology. Even in the dogma most intimately hers, Mary does not come into prominence for her own sake, but for that of her Son. Her human likeness in its psychological details is inaccessible to every historic-critical method, to the most understanding interpretation, even to the most ardent love. It rests veiled in the mystery of God.

It is veiled, however, for the express purpose of disclosing itself in its religious significance, for on earth the veil is the symbol of the metaphysical. It is likewise the symbol of womanhood, and all great forms of woman's life show her as a figure veiled. This makes it clear why the greatest mysteries of Christianity entered the world of creation not through the man, but by way of the woman. The annunciation of the Christmas message to Mary repeats itself in the Easter message to Magdalen, while the mystery of Pentecost reveals man in an attitude of womanly acceptance. The Church indicates this same association of concepts, when at religious services and also at the marriage ceremony she assigns woman to the Gospel side of the altar.

Surrender as a metaphysical mystery, surrender as a mystery of redemption is, according to Catholic dogma, the mystery of woman, rendered visible with unique perfection and surpassing that of every other creature in the image of the Blessed Virgin and Mother, reflected in manifold form as in a tremendous hierarchy of surrender. As the sibyl rises in advance of Mary, so the cosmic mystery precedes the Christian mystery of redemption as though it were prophetic.

The motif of womanhood echoes through all creation. Like a far-off, tender prelude, it hovers above the opened womb of the bridal earth and broods over the fond mother beast of the wilds, which in its motherhood almost breaks its animal barriers. It is poised over the loving bride and wife, suspended in abounding measure over every human mother eclipsed in the radiance of her child. It is recognizable still in the sensuously prodigal mistress and lingers over the most trivial, the most transitory act of giving— upon the smallest, the most childlike kindness, even upon its barest premonition. It mounts from out the natural sphere to that which is spiritual and supernatural.

Wheresoever woman is most profoundly herself, she is not as herself but as surrendered, and wherever she is surrendered, there she is also bride and mother. The nun dedicated to adoration, to works of mercy, to the mission field, carries the title of mother; she bears it as virgin mother. The sibyl who with "foaming lips" announces a new aeon is the mother of that which is to come, for all prophecy is but a form of motherhood. As the sibyl precedes Mary, so the saint succeeds her. In her, the primal mystery returns to the place that is its home.

It is profoundly understandable, therefore, that the most astounding achievements of women have been connected with the sphere of religion. St. Catherine of Siena was entrusted with the task of bringing the Pope from Avignon back to Rome, and she did it. St. Joan of Arc received even the banner of the battlefield; it is especially these extraordinary commitments that woman receives in the manner of a bride, that is, under a veil. It is precisely the veil that is the evidence of every great womanly mission. For this reason St. Catherine of Siena was not present at the Pope's entrance into Rome and St. Joan received her veil in the flames of her funeral pyre.

In keeping with the veil motif, the unpretentious is preeminently proper to woman, which means all that belongs to the domain of love, of goodness, of compassion, everything that has to do with care and protection, the hidden, the betrayed things of the earth. Therefore, the times during which woman is crowded out of public life are not in the least detrimental to her metaphysical significance. On the contrary, it is probably those very periods that, for the most part unknowingly, throw the colossal weight of womanhood into the scales of the world.

Wherever surrender is, there also is a flash from the mystery of the Eternal Woman. But when the woman seeks herself, the metaphysical mystery is extinguished; for in uplifting her own image she destroys the one that is eternal. Only from this point of view does the great defection of the woman become understandable, that is Eve. To seek its reason in the contradiction between the senses and the spirit is of no avail. The defection of woman is not really that of a creature falling earthward; it is rather a descent away from the earth insofar as the earth itself signifies something womanly, something that awaits in humble readiness. The fall in the Paradise story is not contingent upon the temptation through the sweetness of the fruit, nor does it hinge upon the temptation to the knowledge of good and evil; but it is the result of the deceiving promise: "You shall be like unto God", which is the contradiction to the fiat of the Virgin. The actual fall into sin, therefore, occurs in the religious sphere and, consequently, in its most profound sense signifies the fall of woman. This is not because Eve was the first to take the apple, but because she took it as woman. Creation fell in its womanly substance, for it fell in its religious sense. The greater guilt, therefore, can in a sense be ascribed not to Adam but to Eve.

On the other hand it is entirely false to say that Eve fell because she was the weaker. The Bible story shows clearly that she was the stronger and had the ascendancy over man. Man, regarded in his cosmic aspect, stands in the foreground of strength, while woman dwells in its deeper reaches. Whenever woman has been suppressed, it was never because she was weak, but because she was recognized and feared as having power, and with reason; for at the moment when the stronger power no longer desires surrender but seeks self-glorification, a catastrophe is bound to ensue. The dark narrative of the struggle over the tumbling matriarchate still quivers with the fear of woman's power. The most profound surrender has as its opposite the possibility of utter refusal, and this is the negative side of the metaphysical mystery of woman. It is because, according to her very being, and her innermost meaning, she is not only destined to surrender, but constitutes the very power of surrender that is in the cosmos, that woman's refusal denotes something demoniacal and is felt as such. She is never the power of evil in itself; the fallen angel exceeds her in revolt, and the devil is masculine; but she shares his power of seduction. Seduction is self-will, the opposite to surrender. The fallen angel is more terrible than the fallen human being; so also is the woman who falls more terrible than the man in his fall. Her drama is portrayed with overpowering magnificence in Kleist's *Penthesilea*. In the picture of Medusa and that of the Furies the ancient saga also reflects the horror inspired by the woman who has fallen. Even the belief in witches during Christian centuries, however tragically it may have erred in individual cases, signifies in its deeper implications the utter rightness of the aversion against the woman who has become unfaithful to her metaphysical destiny. It is only the monstrous triviality that today exhibits the decline of woman empirically, that fails to arouse a similar horror, for obviously the story of the fall repeats itself continuously. In its deeper sense woman is the cause of every defection, not only because she is the mother within whose womb sinners are formed, but also because every fall, even that of man, is consummated within the sphere that has in a special sense been entrusted to woman.

As woman in her failure stands at the beginning of human history so also she stands at the conclusion of all history. It is not the man who is the apocalyptic figure of the human being; for the essential characteristic of the "latter days" is precisely that the form of the man disappears, since he is no longer capable of controlling the naked forces of destruction in manly fashion. For this reason also, St. John's Apocalypse does not characterize the antichrist as a human being, but as a beast rising out of the abyss. Woman, however, according to St. John, is recognizable as an apocalyptic figure. Only a woman who has become unfaithful to her destiny can portray that absolute unfruitfulness of the world which must inevitably cause its death and destruction.

If the sign of the woman is "Be it done unto me", which means the readiness to conceive or, when expressed religiously, the will to be blessed, then there is always misery when the woman no longer wills to conceive, no longer desires to be blessed. This does not apply only in a biological sense. The ascending line that is the hierarchy of surrender implies a descending line of refusal, and a world yawns between the tragically heroic refusal of the amazon and the apocalyptic refusal of the woman. Just as the man under the sway of naked powers, which he should control, loses his human quality, so the woman loses it as a whore, and it is the "great whore" that is the apocalyptic image of the end of time.

The whore signifies the radical destruction of the fiat when surrender gives place to that last form of inner refusal which is prostitution. The word does not mean a judgment pronounced against an individual from among these poorest of all women; for the whore herself already represents the judgment. She no longer serves in the capacity of one who cooperates in the spirit of humility and love. She serves but as a thing, and the thing avenges itself through domination. Over the man who has fallen under the dominion of dark forces she rises triumphantly, the enslaver of his passions. The whore as utter unfruitfulness denotes the image of death. As mistress she is the rule of utter destruction.

The apocalypse of the final days is preceded by the apocalypses of separate periods and cultural cycles. This is to say of our own day, that religious aberration in unheard-of dimensions is becoming distinctly visible in the empiric manifestation of womanhood. The withdrawal of the veil, like the veil itself, is deeply symbolic. We have said that all the great forms of woman's life show her as concealed. The bride, the widow, and the nun are the bearers of the same symbol. The outer gesture is never without meaning; for, as it issues from a thing, just so does it represent that very thing. From this point of view certain fashions become monstrous traitors; in fact, they contribute to the dismantling of woman in the actual sense of the word. To unveil her means to destroy her mystery.

The woman who does not surrender herself, even in the sphere of the sensuous, and is dedicated only to the most miserable of all cults, that of her own body, and this amid conditions of unspeakable distress among her fellow human beings, represents a degeneration that has torn asunder the last bond with her metaphysical destiny. Here it is no longer the inoffensively childlike face of feminine vanity that is looking at us; in its stead, ghostly and banal, a countenance emerges that denotes the complete opposite to the image of God: the faceless mask of womanhood. This, and not the face of the bolshevist proletarian disfigured by hunger and hatred, is the true expression of modern godlessness. With this, our consideration returns to its beginning, to the revelation of the inviolate image of the divine, in the dogma of the Immaculate Conception.

The proclamation of a dogma is always the response to a definite religious danger. The Marian dogma, as we have observed, when formulated in its most general sense, means the co-operation of a creature in the work of redemption. It is only from this definition that its tremendous meaning in connection with our own times first dawns upon us. Divine grace does not change; it is the cooperation of the creature that in these days in increasing measure gives evidence of change.

It is but the consequence of this teaching concerning cooperation that Mary shines forth as the most powerful help to an endangered faith, as the true conqueror of religious apostasy. It is not accidental that the saints of our own time so frequently achieve perfection by a particular attachment to Mary, nor is it by chance that today theology tends insistently toward an even stronger development of her dogma in the direction of Mediatrix of All Graces. This is what the Litany of Loreto means when it praises Mary as Queen of Angels, including as it does also the fighter-angel, St. Michael. It means this when it elevates her to the title of Queen of Apostles, for she is the one without whom even the apostolic message would not be effective. The invocation "Queen of the most holy Rosary" has the same import, for prayer is not accomplished without the willingness and the readiness of the human heart. The Marian dogma invokes not only the cooperation of the creature in Mary, but also that of the whole universe.

Every religious need, however, is but the source of a more universal distress. The profound connection between godlessness and judgment, namely, the obvious fact that a disturbance in the heart of life must affect all the realms of the outer life, has become lost as a general conviction of our time. On the other hand, however, this age possesses the most magnificent and awe-inspiring evidence of this truth that has ever been given to an era. The belief in Mary as the conquering power against religious apostasy is therefore but the summit of the faith in her as Mother of Perpetual Help.

Woman has, in the utmost sense of the word, been the bearer of salvation. This does not apply to the sphere of religion alone—but because it is true in this sphere, it is valid in general. The idea that nations and countries, if they are to prosper, need good mothers, expresses, in addition to its obvious, biological truth, the deeper reality that the world of the spirit also desires, not only the guidance of man, but like-wise the motherly care of woman. At this point the lines inter-sect. If on the one hand the creature refuses to cooperate with the redemption, it has on the other hand usurped redemp-tion. The faith in self-redemption as man's belief in his own creative powers is the specifically masculine madness of our secularized age and is at the same time the explanation of all its failures. Nowhere is the creature a redeemer, but it should be a cooperator in the work of redemption. Creative power can only be received, and the man also must conceive the creative spirit in the sign of Mary, in humility and sur-render, or he will not receive it at all. In its stead he will admit again and again only the spirit, to use Goethe's words, "that he comprehends" and that in the final analysis can compre-hend nothing; for the world may indeed be moved by the strength of the man, but blessed, in the true sense of the word, it will be only with the sign of the woman.

Surrender to God is the only absolute power that the creature possesses. Only the handmaid of the Lord is the Queen of Heaven. Wherever the creature cooperates with utmost sincerity, there the Mother of the Creator will appear, the Mother of Good Counsel. Wherever the creature becomes detached from self, the Mother Most Amiable, the Mother of Fair Love, comes to the aid of the tortured world. Wherever the nations of the earth are of good will, the Queen of Peace intercedes for them.

The redemption of the inner world, however, is only an image of the redemption from beyond. Again nature sup-plies the prelude for the supernatural, and this prelude ech-oes through all the spheres of being. The bridal earth that opens to the seed receives for its last repose also the thing that dies. As all life rises out of surrender, so also in sur-render it ends. But the earth, which receives the dead, is not itself eternity; it only returns the creature to eternity, and the dying creature itself becomes the seed of a resurrection. Mary is the Patroness of the Dying, the Mother of Mercy. Her figure has a dual aspect. The patroness of the dying person is also the patroness of the dying earth, the earth that at some time will disintegrate. This means that she is the Madonna of the Apocalypse, of whom the Madonna of the Assumption is the anticipation.

The painter El Greco has represented the Madonna of the Apocalypse under the image of the Immaculate Conception. The singularly terrifying and threatened loveliness of the landscape that he places at her feet reflects the atmosphere of the world before the appearance of Christ and is at the same time prophetic of the mood of destruction that will precede his Second Coming. It expresses that groan and travail of the creature that, according to the words of St. Paul, is still in the pangs of birth. Apocalypse is not only a declining; it is also a dawning, and the returning Christ comes in the strength of the Creator of the world. The Madonna of the Apocalypse as the Immaculate Conception signifies the annunciation of a new heaven and a new earth. Mary—Patroness of the Dying, Mother of Mercy—is already the Mother of Divine Grace.

At this point the motif of the Morning Star appears again, the star that heralds the sun yet pales in its presence. Just as the Litany of Loreto, interrupting suddenly its great invocations to Mary, casts itself at the feet of the Lamb of God, so the Eternal Womanhood kneels in the presence of Eternal Divinity. The ultimate mystery of the Immaculata is the Creator. The ultimate mystery of the Co-redemptrix is the Redeemer. And the glory of the Holy Spirit, of Uncreated Love itself, is the crown, but also the veil, the last, the everlasting veil upon the head of the Virgin Mother.

THE WOMAN IN TIME

Woman in time! This apparently would signify fully half of all human existence and activity and therefore the half of history. It is evident, however, that not woman but man and his work form the content of historical life. Not only does man dominate the great political activities of nations, but he also determines the rise and decline of their culture. Furthermore, and this is perhaps the most significant: even life in its religious relationships, which, as we have seen, is in special measure entrusted to woman, has in its large historical manifestations been fashioned by man, and he primarily is its representative.

Whenever one listens for the voice of the centuries, it is his voice that one hears—while woman, with certain exceptions, appears but as the timeless abundance of a living silence which accompanies his voice, or is its carrier. Does this mean that the surrendering power of the cosmos, which is the mystery of woman, implies a further surrender, the renunciation in a metaphysical sense of historical life? Does "religious" mean "powerless", on earth? Shall one say of the religious quality that its kingdom is not of this world? Or do both questions demand that one must reach down to a more profound level? Do they require a new standard of historical evaluation? Here the particular proposition merges with the general problem of the present day, and woman in time becomes a question of the woman of our time.

It is known that in our days the standards of historical evaluation have undergone a transformation. Those of the last epoch were derived largely from the high esteem with which it regarded personality. The general public found its dignity and its value represented in the great individual personality. The present time, on the contrary, presses toward the suprapersonal. It does not deny the significance of the great personality, but it no longer finds an ultimate value in its predominance. Today, the importance of even the greatest individual lies in his surrender to the general welfare, and in the measure of his contribution in this respect, his value is determined. Hence the new standard of historical evaluation is no longer personality, but surrender. From this different perspective the significance of the sexes in the course of history must be examined anew, that is, according to the dominating forces that are their fundamental endowment.

If one inquires into the original laws of life, biological research confirms the assertion that woman does not in herself either represent or exercise the great, historically effective talents, but she is nevertheless their silent carrier. If one wishes to find the source of great personal endowments one must not proceed from sons to their fathers, but to their mothers. To this fact a great number of gifted men and their mothers bear testimony. On the other hand, extraordinary men frequently have insignificant sons. This seems to indicate that man spends his strength in his own performance, while woman does not spend but transmits it. Man spends and exhausts himself in his work and in giving his talent gives himself with it, while woman gives even the talent away to the coming generation. Her endowment appears as equal to that of the man, but it is not for the woman herself; it is for the generation. With this fact, the dominating motif of the present day comes to the surface. Woman's innate endowment is not defined by her personality, which it transcends, and because of this she stands in

alignment with the very factor that constitutes our standard
of value now.

This also imparts a symbolic meaning to the observation
that the woman on average lives longer than the man. The
latter represents the historical situation of his time, while
the woman stands for the generation. Man signifies the eternal value of the moment; woman, the unending sequence
of the generations. Man is the rock upon which the times
rest; woman is the stream that bears them onward. The rock
is formed, the stream is fluid; individual personality belongs
primarily to the man, while universality is the characteristic of the woman. The personal is the unique and therefore
the transient; it consumes its capital, but the universal con-
serves it.

Like the individual woman who in general lives longer
than the individual man, so also the female line of generation survives that of the male. When we say of families
and races that they have died out, we refer as a rule only to
the male branch; the female line frequently continues and
perhaps never becomes extinct. We rarely realize that the
blood of the great families of the past, as for instance the
Hohenstaufens or even the Carolingians, may be traced down
to the present day through the daughter families in which
the name of the male branch has disappeared.

As woman primarily denotes not personality but its surrender, so also the endurance that she is able to give to her
descendants is not self-assertion, but something purchased
at the expense of submerging herself into the universal stream
of succeeding generations. At this juncture we encounter
the second basic motif of woman, that of the veil. Insofar
as she herself is concerned, even the activity most fundamentally her own, the passing on of life and heritage of
blood, remains nameless and concealed. The great stream

of all the forces that have made and will continue to make history proceeds through the woman who bears no other name than that of mother. Our time does justice to this elemental fact when it values woman first of all as mother.

Beside the mother stands the single woman. That the majority of women who cannot become mothers today belong to the generation that has suffered from war is also symbolic. Their hope of fulfillment in marriage, and with it that of man's protection and support, lies buried in the graves of Europe and Asia. The war brings out more strongly what has always and everywhere been the case. So far as the mother is concerned, woman's problem is relatively easy to solve. Nature has already provided the solution; furthermore, all problems of economic need are beyond the range both of nature and of metaphysical reality with which we are here concerned. The inner weight of the question does not bear upon the mother, but upon the unmarried woman.

That our time avoids coming to terms with her is understandable. It entertains the naïve conviction that the significance of the unmarried woman comes to the fore in the bride. From a positive standpoint the age sees her only as girlish expectancy; negatively, she denotes the disappointed old maid or, what is worse, the contented bachelor girl. Consequently our period sees the unmarried woman only as a condition or as something tragic. A mere condition passes away; a tragedy may perhaps be averted in the future. The question here, however, concerns not only a condition, but a value that may be retained even in case of tragedy. The one whom we negatively call the unmarried woman is in a positive sense the virgin. Obviously, she is not the only aspect of the unmarried woman, but she is her most natural expression.

In other times a virgin held a definite position of dignity. Not only does Christianity approve of her, but many of the values that it emphasizes have been anticipated also in pre-Christian times. Names of mountains and of constellations proclaim the virgin, while her character as expressed in a Diana or a Minerva, though differently conceived and motivated, is in a natural sense no less impressive than that of the Christian saint. The exalted honor that the Germanic woman of prehistoric times enjoyed was linked with the appreciation of virginity. To this the terrible, punitive laws of the ancient Saxons bear testimony, when they direct themselves with equal severity against the assault upon the chastity of a virgin and against the crime of the woman who had fallen.

Like the priestess of Vesta, the Germanic prophetess also was a virgin. Both the German saga and the German fairy tale, despite their pagan sources, show us repeatedly the meaning of the virgin who is pure. In the saga she possesses even a redemptive power, and up to the later Middle Ages the irreproachable virgin could obtain pardon for a man condemned to death. She alone could avert the inevitable curse and break a spell of magic that could not otherwise be loosed. To borrow Theodore Haecker's[2] beautiful expression, which he applied to the classical ages, the pagan period of early Germanic history, in its belief in the saving power of a virgin, became "like an advent" preparing the way for the Christian faith in Mary.

The Litany of Loreto calls Mary the Virgin of Virgins and the Queen of Virgins. The Mother of all mothers remains, as mother, the virgin undefiled. By the dogma of

[2] An outstanding German Catholic poet and writer who died in Munich shortly after World War II.

the perpetual virginity of the Mother of God, the Church expresses not only the inviolable purity of Mary, but establishes for all time the independent meaning of virginity in itself, placing its dignity beside the dignity of motherhood.

This concept of virginity that the dogma has worked out enters into the Christian era of great occidental art, illuminating at the same time both the pre- and the post-Christian epochs. Whenever art that was truly great represented the virgin, it did not express a temporary condition such as maidenly expectation, nor did it depict a hope destroyed; it heralded a mystery. In the magnificent sculptures of antiquity as well as during the golden age of Christian plastic and pictorial art, virginity in its most authentic expression appears in an absolute sense. It is not the outward loveliness, the inviolability of aspect, but the inner character that is its secret.

This quality is apparent in poetry even more, if possible, than in great visual art. It is striking to observe how frequently poetry exalts woman in her virginal type rather than in that of wife and mother. Antigone and Beatrice, Iphigenia and Tasso's Princess are virginal figures and can be properly understood only as such. Schiller in his presentation of Joan of Arc did not grasp the idea of the saint; but the concept of virginity he recognized as irrefutable, for the power of her personality is rooted in it. Here the idea of virginity touches upon the masculine quality. The man also values virginity as adding help and intensity to the pursuit of his highest achievement. This is the meaning of the well-known counsel that priests, soldiers, and political leaders, in fact all whose duty it is to devote their lives fully to a certain cause, should remain unmarried.

Thus from dogma, history, saga, and art, the idea of virginity emerges, not as a condition or a tragedy, but as a value and a power. To recognize this, means for our times to face a double difficulty. God no longer stands at the center of its thinking as he did in that of an earlier day. Instead, man has moved into the foreground, not as an individual, but as a link in the chain of generations. The virgin, however, has her place, not within the generation, but at its concluding point. She no longer holds her position on the progressively advancing line of an earthly infiniteness, but she is identified with that single moment of her personal life which seems so limited in time. From this situation she exacts faith in the ultimate value of the individual as such, a value not justified by mere human qualities. In other words, her formal meaning is the religious exaltation and affirmation of a person's value, as directly and ultimately related to God.

Like the solitary flower of the mountains, far up at the fringe of eternal snows, that has never been looked upon by the eye of man; like the unapproachable beauty of the poles and the deserts of the earth, that remain forever useless for the service and the purposes of man, the virgin proclaims that the creature has significance, but only as a glow from the eternal radiance of the Creator. The virgin stands at the margin of the mysteries of all that is apparently wasted and unfulfilled. Like those who have died in early youth and have not lived to unfold their most glorious gifts, she stands at the brink of all that has seemingly failed. Her inviolability, which, if it be purity, always includes a depth of pain, denotes the sacrifice that is the price for insight into the immortal value of a person. This explains why the liturgy always places the virgin beside the martyr, who bears witness to the absolute value of the soul.

From the religious significance of the virgin it becomes clear and imperative that orders of women demand the vow of virginity. In this connection, something else becomes equally evident, namely, that everything temporal derives its real meaning from that which is eternal. Here we come upon the fact that wherever it is advisable to lay the deepest roots of a matter bare, it is the great Catholic dogma that has worked out the determining concept. At this point it is necessary to glance briefly at the religious ceremony for the consecration of virgins. The words of the Preface preceding it are decisive: "While respecting the nuptial blessing resting upon the sacred state of marriage, there should still be noble souls who disregard the physical union entered upon by man and wife, and who give all their love to the mystery suggested by marriage",[3] that is, the mystery of charity.

The mystery of love, therefore, hovers equally over the nuptial Mass and the dedication of virgins; for the consecrated virgin is the spouse of Christ. In agreement with the world, the Church also affirms that the virgin is as one destined to be a bride, but she does not see her only at the side of a man. For one charged moment the profound association between the Marian dogma and every mystery of womanhood becomes strikingly clear. Mary's perpetual virginity signifies the espousal and the overshadowing of the Holy Spirit. This is to say also of the consecration of the virgin that it is her Fiat mihi, her "Be it done unto me", to her unmarried state. On the part of God it is the fulfillment of the virgin's life through the mystery of a charity resting upon a higher plane than the natural. The value of the person as such, which must first be established with regard to every human being, can be established only because such value exists before God, and it is established precisely in the religious mystery of charity. From this assurance a shaft

[3] From an ancient bridal prayer of the *Sacramentarium Fuldense.*

of light descends straight through all the levels of solitary feminine existence. In the language of dogma this denotes the appearance of the vicarious as a concept.

Representation in its religious meaning, translated into secular language, is the cooperating responsibility of all for all. This, in the light of the concept of the Mystical Body of Christ, expresses the religious pinnacle of a thought which our times have undertaken to proclaim far and wide over the secular field, by demanding the conquest of individualism. It is only the lack of true insight into the essence of the dogma, which still clings to our time as heir of a liberal tradition, that bars this age from the consciousness of its own coordination with Christian truth. Just as the work of a creative genius does not belong only to him who fashioned it, so also perfection and the loving deed do not belong only to the perfect one or the loving one; they are the possession of all. Only to a time blinded by subjectivism could it seem impossible that the merits of the saints are able to benefit their brethren upon earth. In application to our theme, this is to say that in similar fashion the mystery of charity inherent in the consecration of virgins streams out upon the world. The idea of the spouse of Christ clarifies the hidden meaning that belongs to every virgin, a significance that even the least and most inconspicuous among them unconsciously defends.

It is here among the least and most inconspicuous that the idea peculiar to our time, that of the unmarried woman as a tragic object, has its place. The involuntary sacrifice stands in contrast to the voluntary one; the mystery of iniquity offsets the mystery of charity; instead of the "be it done unto me" we have the "no" of the creature. For the woman who does not recognize in her virginity a value that has its relationship to God, the unmarried state and childlessness are really a profound tragedy. Both to marriage and to children, woman is spiritually and physically more intimately disposed than man, and to be deprived of them can lead her to regard her own existence as utterly futile. However, the inner meaning of her unmarried state and her childlessness remains unimpaired by this apparent uselessness. In fact, by an extreme sharpening of the concept, it is perhaps exactly at this point that it becomes decidedly intensified; for it is perhaps only an existence seemingly the most worthless that can most fully establish the final value of a person as such. In every other instance there would be danger lest some achievement, and not the personality itself, constitute its ultimate significance.

At this point religious dialectics crosses worldly reasoning. The contemplative life, which regarded from a religious angle gives evidence of man's final destiny in God, when humanly considered means for the most part a lack of achievement in the world. In a similar way the low voice of the solitary woman, whose life in the world has remained unfulfilled, echoes in sisterly fashion the avowal of fulfillment on the part of the spouse of Christ. It is only in the complete release from every visible achievement that we have a glimmer of the ultimate, the transcendental meaning of the person. Here the line swings back into the problem of the present. What does the concept of the person mean to our time? What can it still mean?

Our period has rightfully overcome the meaning of the personality as a single value; nevertheless the excellence of the person should not in any way be questioned. Personality is a temporal value; person is an eternal value. As God himself is a Person, so also Christian redemption concerns the person. It is only through the person that the real meaning and purpose of history is determined. Without eternal values only historical sequence remains. This leads us to the dual significance of woman in history. If it belongs to the meaning of the mother that she transmit man's history-making capabilities into a given generation, it belongs to the virgin first to guarantee these capabilities of man as a person.

If we have acknowledged the religious import of the virgin, we arrive at once at her temporal significance. The very woman who sacrifices marriage and motherhood in order to represent the worth of the solitary person secures by this renunciation both marriage and motherhood. Just as she herself would not remain a virgin if she did not respect the concept of marriage for her own person, so she defends thereby the marriage of her sister women. For the majority of the latter the dissolution of the marriage tie becomes inevitable as soon as the unmarried woman loses her respect for virginity. Without the virgin there is no marriage and therefore no really protected motherhood. She who concludes the generation to render the final worth of the individual person secure likewise guards the safety of the generation, and she does it by very reason of her respect for the value of a person.

As both wedlock and virginity are anchored in the mystery of charity, so are they anchored in the human person upon whose value marriage is fundamentally established. Hence the ultimate worth of the person does not devolve only upon the person, but also upon the generation. If these continuities are practically unknown to the world in general, this again signifies the veil within which all womanly living is concealed. Without this veil these things would obviously lack their final authenticity and hence their most profound power, for decisive results have their source in hidden places.

This brings us face to face with the concept of the virgin as a power. The man also, as we have noted, is aware of the meaning of virginity in his own life, as an intensifying force toward the highest achievement. Every conservation of strength at one point implies the possibility of augmented functioning at another. In this sense virginity is not an exclusion, but rather a rearrangement of abilities for accomplishment. With reference to woman this means that her capacity for love, which finds no possibilities for outlet in a family of her own, transfers itself to the great human family.

When the unmarried woman who cannot render her abilities fruitful through generation uses them for some objective achievement, she does it by the same process of giving that belongs biologically to the mother. And here the concept of virginity touches upon that of spiritual motherhood. This we shall discuss later. We are dealing at the moment with woman in time. The mother, however, and also the spiritual mother, is not bound by time; she is timeless. Therefore the question here concerns itself not with the achievement of woman as a mother in the realm of symbolism, but with her actual spiritual achievement.

Virginity, therefore, denotes in a special manner a capacity, a release for action. This clarifies the reason why the drama that is built entirely upon action so definitely prefers the virginal figure of woman to that of the wife and mother. The same law applies both to the creative writer and to the figure he creates. Consequently not only Antigone and Iphigenia, but also the writers Hroswitha of Gandersheim and Annette von Droste-Hülshoff,[4] are essentially virginal.

Thus the woman whose forces are unfettered by the duties of generation, who feels herself impelled to use her power

[4] Annette von Droste-Hülshoff: A German mystic, and a German poetess.

for the purpose of cooperating in the historical and cultural life of her people, finds a profound justification. The more so is this justified since the form of this cooperation is largely determined by the experience that woman always comes to the rescue when there is need. This historical and cultural activity repeats in the field of objective achievement that which holds good in the field of generation: when the male line fails, the daughter becomes the heir. The need of woman coming to the rescue indicates that too many other demands are being made of man, or that there is some lack of man power, a fact of which the home front of women in world wars has given unforgettable evidence.

The independent advance of woman into the cultural field is, therefore, always significant. Hereupon the face of the eternal woman becomes visible for a moment, above the woman in time, for woman coming to the rescue means, in its strictest sense, that her action is not activity in itself, but surrender, which is but another form of the womanly "Be it done unto me". From this it follows that the activity of woman withdraws of its own accord, when the need for it no longer exists. In this circumstance woman's objective achievement finds its extraordinary, its largely thankless, therefore deeply veiled, recognition; but it finds there also its limitations. This is to say that the significance of woman in historical and cultural life cannot basically be dependent upon her objective cooperation; it is much more profound than this.

Just as the virgin as such stands at the border of the mystery enshrouding all the apparently wasted and unfulfilled things of life, so she stands at this same margin as a person capable of achievement. The veil motif recurs with the fact that, in the order of achievement, woman's contribution so far as the great majority is concerned can occupy at best only a secondary place, since it but seldom exhausts the full depth and power of the feminine soul and allows her to become an independently feminine cultural factor. For the most part she adjusts herself to masculine standards and by this very adjustment is outdistanced by man's original achievement. The veil motif is still discernible, however, when woman actually does attain to some ultimate point of originality and sublimity in her performance, for then the impression of a charismatic vocation is stronger than in the work of a man. The charismatic character of a talent or an activity signifies not only its extraordinary, but primarily its religious quality. It is therefore not fortuitous when genius that is essentially feminine appears only in the religious sphere. No woman of the secular world can measure up to the greatness of a Hildegard von Bingen, a Joan of Orleans, a Catherine of Siena. From this it is conceivable that the very Church which has made man the exclusive carrier of her hierarchy should acknowledge the feminine charisma.

The actual illumination of the matter, therefore, comes from the religious point of view. The concept, spouse of Christ, has clarified the meaning of virginity. In the same way, the essential quality of the work of feminine genius is rendered understandable by the charismatic idea. God alone can lift the veil under which he himself has hidden woman, and even this revelation would mean a more profound concealment. Charisma does not mean the power of working out one's own achievement; it means, on the contrary, to obliterate the person to the point of becoming an instrument of God.

While heretofore we considered the value of the person as apart from any achievement, now by the charismatic vocation, we are implying an achievement as separated from the person who accomplishes it. Charisma itself becomes a veil.

Woman's natural capacity of leaping into a breach becomes, on a loftier level, the fact of woman being called; and, furthermore, she is called only in extraordinary, even desperate cases. The highest vocation of woman is always by way of a last expedient, and we grasp the astonishing significance of a St. Catherine or a St. Joan only when we know who had already failed on the missions that later became theirs.

By the same token by which an existence, worthless according to the standard of achievement, illustrates the ultimate value of the person, so the essential characteristic of a vocation is demonstrated where apparently there is no vocation. It is only in regard to a person that seemingly has no inward call that the character of the bearer of a vocation shows forth with utmost clarity. This sheds light upon the reason why the greatest figures in the history of the world were precisely those who at the beginning of their respective careers seemed insignificant or unfit in the eyes of their contemporaries, and why their importance revealed itself late or despite all expectations. As the humanly valuable is always in danger, at the final issue, of signaling only the value of some achievement and not that of the person who accomplished it, so in the matter of a supreme vocation there is equal danger lest the emphasis be not upon the vocation, but upon the degree of endowment possessed by the person in question. This would mean that the latter were promoting not only his assignment but himself.

In every great achievement there is, however, an added quality that surpasses not only the capabilities, but even the original intentions of the person responsible for it. In other words, it is the splendor of the divine creative will shining through the human achievement that constitutes its actual criterion. As proof of this the person who apparently has no vocation must sometimes turn out to be the very one who is chosen. The invisible pillar of that which has come to pass must be rendered visible. This is the symbolic meaning of the charismatic woman. The basic reason that she, in preference to the man, has been chosen lies in the fact that by nature her personality is more easily able to efface itself into becoming a mere instrument or receptacle. To bear the charisma means to be the handmaid of the Lord.

Thus even woman's most amazing achievement, which is charismatic, lies entirely within the boundaries of the feminine, along the line of mere cooperation, along the path of Mary. Precisely because of this she uplifts the lesser achievement of her insignificant sister-woman. Upon her she sheds the ray of light fallen upon herself from the luminous mystery of the Eternal Woman. The concept of the vicarious appears once more: the sisterly colloquy between the spouse of Christ and the unfulfilled woman in the world continues.

The character of mere cooperation that is evident also in the charismatic woman serves to illumine the mystery of why feminine achievement that is not charismatic inevitably occupies a second or third place. The reason does not hinge upon the question of whether or not one is more or less gifted; it lies in the nature and in the task of woman. That which we have said about the value of the person is valid also in this instance. A final tapering of the thought discloses the inconspicuous achievement as constituting the actual mystery of woman, her meaning not as a visible, but an invisible support of historical life.

As the virgin represents the inherent value of the person as independent of every achievement, so woman as here considered demonstrates the final value of her every gift, her every achievement, entirely independent of success or recognition. She expresses the most complete reality also of the unknown, the seemingly ineffectual, the hidden, as it is in God. Therewith she secures, as do the lone graves of a lost war, the final import of all history. Above and beyond the visible world, she answers for the invisible.

The concept of cooperation, however, opens a further vista. If the teaching of the Church concerning the virgin flows into the idea of the spouse of Christ on the one hand, on the other it opens into that of the spouse of man. The same mystery that hovers over the consecration of a virgin broods also, as we have already seen, over the nuptial Mass. "O Lord our God," we read in an old marriage prayer, "You have willed that for the continuance of the human race one generation should be created from another through the mystery of charity." This mystery of charity, here interpreted as a mystery of creation, is designated in secular language as the creative meaning of the polarity between masculine and feminine forces. Upon the principle of their cooperation all life depends, and the field of their power ranges over all things, even over the domain of intellectual creation.

The question no longer concerns the independent cultural achievement of woman, but her role in cooperation with man, her place within his work. It concerns the acceptance of a mystery of charity also with regard to cultural and spiritual things, and the recognition of the nuptial character of culture. At this juncture an apparent difficulty arises. According to a strict analogy with the natural mystery of creation, spiritual conception and birth should also belong to the woman. She would then stand in the character of mother to the work of man. The mystery of charity however, as a nuptial mystery, is not yet that of the mother, but of the bride, and the bride stands between the virgin and the mother.

These two concepts united in Mary's title as the Eternal Woman, in the magnificent landscape into which dogma places woman, constitute the twin summits or basic pillars between which a wide, fruitful valley stretches out; it is the realm belonging to woman as the companion to man. It is an independent domain, and as we view it we must realize the importance of establishing clearly that every one of these three timelessly valid forms of woman's life—virgin, bride, and mother—implies the fulfillment of woman's life in its entirety, but each within its own proper scope. The association between the separate forms, their merging one into the other, does not indicate a contingency through which, perhaps, the essentially womanly role would fall only to the mother. The bride is, to be sure, the first step to the mother; but she is likewise the bearer of an independent feminine mystery.

The Church expresses this fact inasmuch as she recognizes the childless marriage also as entirely valid and indissoluble. This means that the bride as standing between the virgin and the mother is not only the future bearer of the generation, but as bride she is primarily a person. The sacramental character of marriage does not only consecrate the generation, but it unites a person to a person. It is consequently not solely a matter of the propagation of the race, but concerns also the welfare inherent in the mutual love of two human beings, their spiritual responsibility one for the other, on the way to God.

Therefore the mystery of charity in the nuptial Mass intimates not only the corporal, but also the spiritual fruitfulness of marriage. According to the interpretation of the Church, man and wife are not only of one flesh, but also of one spirit. The bride who in one direction of her being represents the future mother retains on the other hand, not in a natural but in a spiritual sense, the virginal character. She retains it as bride.

It is the bride who signifies the true mystery of the spouse or wife, and as she is an independent mystery so is she also a permanent one. Popular custom does not err in designating the wife of the silver wedding as still a bride. Although she be a mother, the woman, insofar as she is directed toward the love of the man, retains her bridal character. To see in the bride nothing more than the maiden of the wedding day is to give the mystery a purely naturalistic interpretation. In her attitude toward the man who loves her, the wife remains a bride throughout her life. In similar fashion the wedding day repeats itself as long as life lasts, and the bridal quality of the woman corresponds to love in its unending renewal.

From the character of the virgin-spouse, as expressed in the Bride of Christ, a reflected splendor falls also upon the spouse of a man. Upon her also, out of the concept of eternal bridals, the face of Mary the Eternal Woman rises; for Mary, whose title alone unites the Virgin and the Mother, is the Bride of the Holy Spirit. She is, however, also the one who, on Pentecost morning in the company of the Apostles, receives the Holy Spirit. Scripture calls the Holy Spirit both the Spirit of Love and the Creator Spirit, and from this dual designation the twofold character of the mystery of charity grows clear.

Here, as everywhere, we see that the Church has worked out the decisive points of view. As the spouse of Christ illuminates and is the apex of the problem of virginity, so the wife, sacramentally bound, constitutes the culminating point of the spousal concept. Behind her, the immense fullness of creative potentiality between man and woman extends in its spiritual lines to the wife not sacramentally bound, to the woman friend of a man, to his mistress, to the associate of his work. Upon all of them streams the light of the bridal

Mass. The creative significance for salvation that two people have for one another in the shadow of the sacrament becomes in the secular sphere a creative companionship, the unique spiritual meaning of two people for one another. There is also a mystery of charity that belongs to the natural sphere, a mystery of spiritual creation, between a man and a woman; there is also a spouse who is the bride of man's spirit.

Since we are dealing with the cultural, we are approaching those celebrated companionships that will facilitate a vivid consideration of the idea. In this region of thought Dante and Beatrice, Michelangelo and Vittoria Colonna, Hölderlin and Diotima, Goethe and Madame von Stein, Richard Wagner and Mathilda Wesendonk, among others, point the way.

> Through my eyes you entered into me,
> And forced me thus, to grow to mighty stature,

Michelangelo wrote in one of his sonnets to Vittoria Colonna. Hölderlin expresses this thought even more distinctly to Diotima:

> Marveling I look upon you; I hear voices and
>   sweet song
> As from a former time, and the playing of a violin;
> Freed into flames our winging spirits
> Open into air.

The ego has expanded into the we; the consciousness of a dual creativeness becomes evident; the character of spiritual creation emerges as life, the bridal character of culture.

Woman's part in this spiritual mystery of charity is the same as it is throughout historical and cultural life. Only in rare cases does this cooperation become fruitful for the woman in a creation of her own, as for example Elizabeth

Barrett Browning's *Sonnets from the Portuguese* or Marianne Weber's[5] magnificent description of the life and work of her husband. Woman for the most part vanishes in the creative work of man or becomes visible only in the homage thereby offered to her. Of the complete disappearance of even a highly gifted woman into a man's lifework, Marianne von Willemer[6] is an outstanding example; for we know that her participation in the poems of the *Westöstlicher Divan* is greater than we can accurately determine. Fundamentally, however, there is no need to define so active a part played by a woman, for the very fact that she does not as a rule cooperate actively, the better expresses the essential character of her participation.

The spouse concept in its character of bride of the masculine spirit affirms that the spouse as the other part of man constitutes the other half of being as a whole. The wondrous expression found in the Bible, that the man must "know" the woman, applied also to spiritual creation. In her he recognizes the other dimension of human existence. Polarity is totality and is the prerequisite of every great work. Only from this angle does Hölderlin's almost terrifying avowal to Diotima become understandable:

> When the God who inspires me
> Dawns for me upon her brow.

Actually it is not "the God" who dawns; the wholeness of divine creation dawns, the other half of existence without which even "the God" cannot inspire a supremely great work. This is the exalted meaning in Dante's journey from hell to heaven when at the outset the man, Virgil, leads

---

[5] Marianne Weber: Outstanding German sociologist.
[6] Friend of Goethe.

him, and later Beatrice, the beloved of his youth, becomes his guide. One cannot say of this other dimension that it actually manifests itself, but rather that it gives itself. The man knows the woman, and the woman is known by her attitude of surrender.

On the spiritual plane with which we are concerned, it is not a question of taking up a man's thoughts through the mediacy of a woman, nor of a spiritual cooperation and joint development. This may happen now and then, but it remains only a form of the mystery of charity and not its essence. It does not mean, furthermore, merely an understanding accord on the part of the woman; this would be only like a musical accompaniment. But here surrender is revelation; it is a gift. The woman, having surrendered herself to the man, under whatever form, brings to him the dowry of half a world. In the surrender of the woman as a revelation of this other hemisphere consists her participation in man's cultural creation. Surrender is a revelation, but a hidden one. Even in the other world Beatrice is at first veiled as she approaches Dante.

The revelation of the woman is so deeply concealed that there are times when the man utterly fails to recognize it as such. He believes himself to be envisioning not the woman, but his own image. "Then I know that I exist", Hölderlin says of Diotima's nearness. It is only in becoming aware of the other's image that one's own is capable of assuming form. Each has its rightful position only within the whole of creation, and in the light of woman's nature man's being also grows fully clear. Totality does not mean the revelation only of the other half of being; it means the disclosure also of one's own half. As the woman may be known by the man when he approaches her with profound love, so it is only in her love that he completely knows himself. This is the significance of the symbolic mirror that so often appears in the testimony great writers give to their relationship to woman. Dante looks into this mirror when, on the Mountain of Purgatory, Beatrice asks for his profession of faith. This helps one to understand the ardor with which a man has often struggled for a woman, and for her spiritual nearness; it is her spiritual person that includes the tremendous dowry that he can share through her alone.

The bride, as she stands between the virgin and the mother, stands also between person and generation, advancing a step, however, beyond the boundaries of the former. If the virgin has secured to man that final and solitary cultural value, the person, then the bride secures for him the cooperation of half a world. As she rescues his life from its loneliness she also draws him spiritually across the limits of his own person. With the presence of the womanly quality, the anonymous element that is in every great creative work becomes clear.

Here also the elements essential to all that is womanly come to the surface, the character of cooperation, and that of the veil. To express it in another way: in the anonymous element that is present in culture we recognize again the invisible pillar or support of human history. Woman is not the operative but the cooperative influence; the cooperative, however, is also the cocreative. This line of thought obviously demands a definite consideration of the nature of spiritual creation.

With apparent justification one might raise the objection that there is no difference between the object of a creation and the subject of the author; therefore, that the mere inclusion of woman in the work of man does not as yet mean cocreation. This, however, is a comment from the past and the times of the great ego. Today, on the contrary, we do not see in an individual work only the creation of its author; we expect of a great work of art that it be the meeting place of many streams of influence. Our epoch expresses this awareness by the importance it attaches to the landscape, the ground so to say, from which a great work is drawn. The author or artist is the speaker for a chorus that is mute. Not only does he create, but through him something is created. The true author knows that his object creates with him. He is aware of its mysterious entrance into him, of its communications to him, often bordering upon the wondrous. Not only does he love his material; it is as though his material loves him. Dante writes:

> Not always is the artist's striving meet
> to mould the work to fit his spirit's vision,
> To give the substance answer when the thing is deaf.

The artist's vanity or jealousy is therefore always the betrayer of a person who is not in the great sense creative. The truly creative person would refuse to be honored as the sole author of his work. To him it is plain that its grandeur and its range depend upon the participation of many. In this, Richard Wagner's famous words find their meaning: "German people, it is you who have created, who have composed this work!"

This helps us to understand the homage, often rapturous, that great artists have offered to woman. It is a tribute of jubilation in the consciousness of not working alone. It is true, furthermore, that every profound and genuine womanly personality that the work of man presents is a fundamental acknowledgment of the mystery of charity.

The creative procedure between the individual genius and the woman who cooperates with him repeats itself in all the corporate forms of cultural life. In this respect the history of Catholic religious orders as bearers of culture is enlightening. As the spiritual mystery of charity hovers over the great religious friendships of a St. Francis of Assisi and a St. Clare, St. John of the Cross and St. Teresa of Avila, St. Francis de Sales and St. Jane Frances de Chantal, it rests in a similar way upon the foundations associated with these names. The essence of the mystery is not only love, but charity. Every great religious order of men as a carrier of culture has sought and found a sister order for its completion. The *opus Dei* of the Benedictine, the giving of glory to God, which at the same time expresses the indispensable condition and the meaning of all culture, could never have realized its purpose of vicarious praise on behalf of all creation, if the woman's voice were missing in the choir. The Order of St. Francis, which by a new spirit of love and poverty counteracted a culture smothered with luxury, was by its very ideals directed toward the woman's spirit of renunciation and her willing heart. The asceticism and mysticism of St. Dominic finds it supreme fulfillment, not alone in the thought of St. Thomas Aquinas or in Master Eckhart's depth of soul, but also in the activity of St. Catherine of Siena.

And Carmel, which in accord with our present train of thought preeminently denotes the inner freedom that assigns culture to its proper place by obviating from it the danger of becoming an idol, is from its very beginning, by its intimate relation to Mary, founded upon the participation of woman. Even the Society of Jesus, which did not seek a feminine counterpart, was forced to find it insofar as it became the vehicle of the last type of culture that was of European rank, the baroque. A counterpart in a sister society, as St. Ignatius foresaw, could never succeed perfectly. The religious foundations of women built upon the Jesuit ideal of education show only certain ones of its traits. It is the solitary Christian woman not in religious surroundings who comes nearest to the heroic impulse fundamental to this order, which is not protected by monastic enclosure, and nearest also to the unqualified dedication of the individual members to their widely divergent duties. As Carmel demonstrates the capacity for silent suffering that is in woman, so in this instance we have woman's quiet yet heroic defense of the Christian world. Hence also over the Society of Jesus, remote as it is from the ideal of the cloistral family, the mystery of charity arises.

It is poised also over the thousand totally secular associations in which men and women work together. Since they do consist of man and woman they do not represent merely a community of work, but also and always a relevancy to the totality of being. Even this last kind of association is related to the first, if only as conclusion.

Every sort of cooperation, even the most insignificant, between man and woman is, in its bearing upon the wholeness of life, of far greater import than associations that are purely masculine or purely feminine. The latter have their definite purposes, naturally, and they are mostly combative or disciplinary and serve for the development of certain new ideas, always, however, within limited spheres. To culture they are of no importance; in fact they carry the danger of being unfruitful because of narrowness or one-sidedness.

Even some separate works of great creative value, although they seem to contradict this, have never wholly escaped this danger. To this the restriction of their influence to specially chosen spheres testifies, for the exclusive circle inevitably implies a lacking wholeness. There are, of course, certain isolated works of merit beyond the charged field of polarity, but, again, there is no totality. The force of polarity has been the support of all the great epochs of cultural power. The outstanding period of German genius, for instance, corresponds to the Ottonian, which is in turn the most magnificent era of woman's influence in German history. This period is contemporary also with the zenith epoch of the German people.

On the other hand, occasional periods of decadence make temporary limitations naturally understandable, as, for instance, the all but heroic times that gave rise in some European countries to the so-called leagues of men. These indicate the desire for a strong and clean-cut emergence of the masculine pole and imply an aversion to the effeminate man as well as to the masculine woman. That a league of men cannot supply higher standards of culture is obvious, but it can bring about a turning away from certain phenomena that no longer come into question as polar forces of culture. One of the principal obligations of the present is to open up new potentialities for culture on the basis of a new point of view on the part of the man as well as on that of the woman.

These potentialities will first of all coincide with natural conditions: with marriage, friendship, and with associations in one's work. Beyond this, however, the duty of a renewed spirit of companionship must be recognized. It is in this field, which today has grown so unfruitful, that the strength of the period of German genius lay. It is imperative to find anew the indissoluble connection between the form and the formation of life, and to understand that the cultural significance of companionship inheres in the meeting of man and woman on the spiritual plane. It is the expression of such a spiritual intercourse when Herder writes of his meeting with Angelika Kaufmann in one of the social circles of Rome and describes her as "one of the silent, modest graces who lifted up the whole of nature and the people".

Thus the essential aspect of that which is womanly is by its nature determined from the vantage point of both beholder and beheld, and their potentialities extend through all the spheres of human existence. Dante's Beatrice and Strindberg's demoniacal feminine personalities, beyond the abyss that separates them, represent the same totality of being, whether plunged in light or darkness, whether on the way to Paradise or to damnation. This indicates that the mystery of charity between man and woman may also be distorted into a mystery of iniquity. Even the distortion, along the line of creative culture, signifies fruitfulness; but that which emanates from it bears a destructive character.

In this fact lies the enormous responsibility that results from the relations between man and woman. To see it solely in the light of generation and morals is to grasp this responsibility only by half. That which applies to a new living being in the biological sense is true also of the life being produced by artistic or spiritual creation. Here is a focal point that indicates the fully shared responsibility of woman as far as culture is concerned. Her image as reflected in the creative work of man, whether in its exaltation or in its debasement, is the very image that she herself presents to him.

The total results of our considerations thus far illustrate the fact that the questioning with which we approached the problem of woman in time was correct only in a qualified way. Our point of departure was a culture that in its apparent forms is masculine. The essence of culture, however, is the essence of all that lives, and it is therefore bound to the laws of living things, to the combined activity of the powers of polarity permeating all creation. It is precisely from this position that the essence of culture as a life of the spirit finds its boundaries.

When the artist looks out upon the great living, creative reaches of culture, he sees philosophy, poetry, sculpture, even culture itself, in unison with the language of cultured nations, represented in allegorical feminine figures. Thus the womanly aspect against the objective background of the reality of life becomes evident to man, even though veiled, as the concept of the cooperation of woman, in all these creative realms. This indicates that in these domains, consciously or unconsciously, man is in relationship to the totality of being.

It is significant, on the other hand, that in the sections of cultural life where the struggle is keen, where the spirit works in one-sided construction, designations such as materialism, socialism, and futurism have a masculine connotation. It is as though man, when he established these divisions, felt himself alone within them and named them in a manner suited to his gender. Perhaps it is from this direction that creative culture in the sense of something that is alive may determine its limits. It is clear that in its actual abundance it unfolds itself in the places where it continues to include the wholeness of existence, where the mystery of charity is still felt and being accepted. Beyond it, obviously, there are still astonishing achievements, but they approach another order of things. They are no longer in the fullest sense organic creations from a totality of polaric powers; but here the great stream of culture, tumbling in cascades as it were, begins to rush toward the shores where mysteries are no longer needed, and the last remnants of culture end in mere civilization.

Here we come upon further enlightenment. The presence of the feminine impetus means, as we have seen, that of a hidden influence, a helpful, a cooperating, a ministering one. The impulse of reverence belongs to woman. To determine the boundaries of a living culture by the presence of the mystery of charity means to do so by the quality of reverence, and this is but another name for the veil motif.

Civilization, on the contrary, is visible through and through; in place of the motif of reverence we have that of the dominating spirit. Civilization does not include cooperation; it merely makes enchained and soulless powers serviceable. The boundaries of culture as traced by the absence of the womanly element coincide necessarily with the line where the absence of the religious element begins.

The religious element, as said before, does not mean the divine, but it denotes reverence for the divine, and therefore, first of all, humility. The modern world withdraws in terror from this virtue as from the epitome of all that is unworthy. This is a misconception. The opposite of humility is not dignity but pride, which is an exaggeration of the true dignity of a man and therefore leads back toward that which is unworthy of him. Humility, on the contrary, is the innate dignity of man in the presence of God. So far as creativeness is concerned, the religious quality expressed as humility is meant to help us understand how all accomplishments of man on the natural level are for the religious man but a cooperation of the creature under the perspective of religion. Only in this connection are we able to discern the deeper meaning in Hölderlin's exuberant confession:

> When the God who inspires me
> Dawns upon your brow ...

The dominating creative qualities of man are but one part of a productive reality; the other is humility. The dawning of the other dimension of existence is at bottom the dawn of the humility of the creature. This is the great condition for the dawning upon man of God the Creator, the

God who inexorably works only from the two spheres of being. In the cooperation of woman as the mate of his spirit, man experiences his own creativeness as mere cooperation in the work of God, who creates alone.

Only in this connection does that which we called the anonymous element in every great cultural creation become comprehensible. If the names of the great architects of our romanesque cathedrals are for the most part unknown to us, or if we can no longer recognize the figure of the builder behind his work, this does not by any means indicate only that the period was lacking in a sense of personal tradition. It denotes primarily the consciousness that every great work, even on its transcendental side, contains an added element of mystery that extends beyond its natural creator.

As all these cathedrals were built for God's glory alone, so at the same time, in the consciousness of their builders, they were built by God. Before man was able to construct them, God had produced their image in the mind of man. In the anonymity of these great builders, man as it were follows in the footsteps of woman and before God becomes as nameless as she. In this anonymity he finds the other side of his creativeness, and we begin to recognize in the surpassing magnificence of the cathedrals the real and final meaning of the anonymous. If hitherto it appeared as a collaborating element, it here discloses itself also as a cocreating one.

Furthermore, the sublimity of these cathedrals portrays the mystery by which the work proclaims God's creative power on the one hand, and on the other conceals it. God is hidden—a silent, an invisible God. In his creation, he remains in a sense anonymous. This helps us to comprehend our previous assertion, that the power which collaborates also cocreates. Woman, therefore, as the hidden collaborator, represents the anonymity of God; she represents it as the one side of all that is creative. Man, however, participates in this quality insofar as he is in alignment with woman's activity; for only in the working together of both the anonymous and the perceptible forces is the totality of creativeness consummate.

The tremendous meaning of the anonymous, which our time has readily recognized along secular lines, not only emanates from the religious concept, but is rooted in it. Once more, and in its most profound sense, the dual character of the mystery of charity becomes apparent, and the reason why it rests equally upon the nuptial Mass and the consecration of the virgin grows clear. The bride of man is called likewise to be the bride of Christ.

By the same token the meaning of the anonymous element in creative culture hinges upon the religious significance of woman. This is what Léon Bloy expresses with the words *"plus une femme est sainte, plus elle est femme."* This is to say: "The holier a woman is, the more she is a woman." This also is Dante's meaning in that wondrous passage of his great poem when he looks upon Beatrice while her eyes remain steadfastly fixed upon God. Here Dante does not see the divine in woman, but he sees God because her glance is upon God. This is the religious significance of woman and at the same time the meaning of the love between man and woman, recognized and portrayed in its ultimate depths. Here the symbol of the mirror, which so often appears in poetry, rises to its highest potentiality; here the bewildering and sublimely conceived words of Hölderlin come to actual fulfillment. Woman, who along the broad lines of earthly import denotes the union of all creation, on the higher plane signifies also the glance toward the Creator. Totality in a natural sense reaches out beyond itself toward the totality of the supernatural.

The masculine element alone, even the human element by itself, does not suffice. Only in the collaboration of God and man that ultimate and all-embracing totality appears which is the prerequisite of every masterpiece. That which applies to the single work must naturally be true also of culture in its entirety.

This concludes the second hypothesis of our introduction. The religious element is not, as we questioned it above, a powerless one; it is, on the contrary, the concealed strength of all culture.

From this it follows inescapably that nothing is more closely related to the downfall of culture than its utter earthiness; no other influence forces it more closely against the limits of mere civilization. A comparison with the creative works of the past will teach us effectually what culture is when religious, and what it is when unreligious. The staggering disparity between the work of Dante, Cervantes, Shakespeare, or even that of Goethe and Kleist, and the European literature of the past few decades, finds its causes not so much in the lesser creative endowment of more modern writers as in the sundering of these talents from the necessary conditions of their fuller development. Thereby they lack the vision of that farther horizon which alone is able to save culture from giving an impression of intolerable deficiency and utter senselessness.

Talents may be increased, but they can also wither. When the substance has reference to totality, it yields inevitably the breadth and the greatness that give a totality also of form. The actual paradox inheres in the fact that it is the self-seeking, the purely worldly culture that falls into decadence, while that which reaches out beyond itself attains to an immortal affirmation, a participation in the eternity to which a religious motivation uplifts it.

From this dual totality it follows, furthermore, that the betrayal of the mystery of charity is always twofold. These questions are inextricably interwoven. The artist who no longer gives God the honor, and instead proclaims only himself, must, in excluding the religious element from culture, practically eliminate also its womanly quality. In making only his own demands upon culture, man breaks the totality of existence apart, on the immanent as well as on the transcendental side.

In this connection new light falls upon a declining culture that manifests itself also as morally decadent. Marital infidelity and divorce appear but as other forms of separation between man and woman and are directly related also to their spiritual separation, not only because they undermine art with elements of disintegration, but in a much more profound sense. Marital infidelity symbolizes and divorce legalizes the betrayal of the mystery of charity. In man's exclusive claims upon culture he rejects the bride of his spirit in the same manner with which he deserts his wife by infidelity and divorce. Henceforth he stands alone, while culture enters the epoch of these ominous and unfruitful separations which, without recognition of the more underlying causes, the present day brands as individualism. The isolation of the individual, which it rightfully deplores and condemns, is but the result of a fundamental cleavage in the world, the last slow beat, as it were, of a tidal wave of immeasurable range.

For cultural life, then, the absence of the one half of existence has an import similar to that which heresy means for the Church. Heresy is always the outcome of one-sidedness and isolation. By substituting a part for the whole, and making that part absolute, it falsifies the truth. Again the image of the Eternal Woman becomes visible over the destiny of the woman in her times: Mary, according to the teaching of the Church the conqueror of heresy, restores through the mystery of charity the totality that God wills.

During the epochs when a one-sided, masculine culture prevails, not only are all feminine characteristics absent, but faith in the hidden forces is replaced by confidence in bare evidence, be it power in material affairs or a kind of advertisement in things of the spirit. Such a culture means, furthermore, an excess of masculine characteristics, and their disfigurement in the face of the man who stands alone. The absence of one part of reality, and this is extremely important, calls forth a strange unsteadiness in the image of the remaining part.

"Only where most I am yours, am I entirely my own", Michelangelo writes in his sonnets to Vittoria Colonna. The exaggeration of masculine traits in cultural life expresses negatively the validity of his words. Every image, as we have already emphasized, finds its meaning and its mission only within the totality. Basically, the very epochs that exclude woman from their cultural life manifest in a negative, yet nonetheless impressive fashion, their own especial need of her. Consequently, man's intention to eliminate or suppress woman never represents the real misfortune, for in this instance his opinion touches only facts and not the essential question. Even the rejected wife retains her nuptial character and is, in her banishment, immeasurably significant. As wife she nevertheless continues to stand in the eternal order of woman's life, as the other half of man. It is then that the sacrament of matrimony, as the highest form of the mystery of charity and its actual consecration, stands forth in its inflexible sublimity and in the fullness of its sacred character, precisely at the moment when the marriage is most endangered.

The divorced woman remains a wife and the other part of the man, because she is so before God. It is in the indissolubility of sacramental marriage that the part of the sexes within the cosmos is mirrored. Metaphysically considered, this indissolubility denotes the inseparable quality of the two adjoining spheres of being, and the primal fact that God has established the one half of existence as irrevocably feminine.

Man's rejection of woman, however, never results without a participation in guilt on her part. Far worse than the man who desecrates the spiritual mystery of charity is the woman who disrupts the divine ordering of her life. In this respect the period recently passed is extremely enlightening. One has tried to pass the judgment upon it that woman had become masculine, but this is to regard the matter only superficially. It is true that woman did at the time possess the greatest possibilities of staking everywhere the full weight of her womanly character, and yet today the opinion prevails that, although in the recent past, she has become visible, she has not been fundamentally effective.

This is not a criticism of the individual woman, nor even an unqualified one of the period. "He who does not reverence his past", says Richard Wagner, "has no future." As seen from a certain distance, epochs sometimes approach one another in startling fashion. That future generations may look upon our age as indebted to the very period that we so frequently condemn is quite conceivable. We still share its belief that it is a given surface condition that matters, while basically the issue depends upon the essential factor that controls these conditions.

There will be occasion, furthermore, to prove that the emergence of woman, as demonstrated by the period recently past, has resulted from a profound break in the womanly character. The religious bond uniting the family was largely destroyed and with it the primal sphere of woman. This sphere had still offered even to the unmarried woman the possibility for an absolute fulfillment so long as it left the view toward ultimate values open to her.

The feminist movement had its spiritual roots in the dullness and the narrowness of the middle-class family. Its economic backgrounds do not concern us here. From the need of their unfulfilled souls the women of that period cried out for spirit and for love. Herein lies their profound and respect-commanding tragedy. They sought for inclusion into the man's world and sought it outside the family, which could no longer accept them and be their fulfillment.

To the dull and narrow-minded middle-class family corresponded a national and an international family which, through the dissolution of the religious bond, had likewise been largely destroyed. This destruction coincided with new and unheard-of obligations toward security of existence and of culture. The woman of that time, ready to help, plunged into this cauldron of distress and struggle that affected both bodies and souls because it was the result of a loss of balance, spiritually no less than materially, of both the individual and the masses. From the experience of her own distress, woman found her way to the universal need, and to the concept of participation in social responsibility. This will remain forever as a page of honor in her history.

Like almost every great and vital thought of the present day, this idea of sharing responsibility is a Christian heritage; for we have already recognized in the idea of the vicarious its originally sacred character. As viewed in this conjunction, which as yet is scarcely perceptible, the positive, truly womanly impulse that gave rise to the feminist movement becomes clear. At once the reason becomes equally plain why the results of this impulse necessarily remained far in arrears of all hopes and expectations. The fate of the feminist movement represents but part of the destiny of the epoch. It was bound to be what it was; for, instead of renewing the foundations of social life, it strove to reinforce the outer walls of the edifice. The very intrusion of the social question as an independent one indicates a certain degradation of culture, for only spiritual resources, not merely social means, are able to regulate the social order.

Instead of tackling the cultural problem under a fundamental perspective, the struggle centered on preliminary and secondary issues. Instead of saving, above all, the spirit itself, one felt obliged primarily to secure only its potentialities. At the base of the general distress that woman discovered in the world lay the same need that had driven her out of the family. She could, to be sure, bring her strength to bear upon spiritual and social matters; whether or not she could inject her true nature into them depended, in the exterior world that she now entered as before in the family, solely upon her attitude toward the eternal order of existence.

Woman can establish the womanly quality only as carrier of the womanly symbol; and her symbol is the veil, the sign of espousal. The cultural role of the woman adhering to the eternal order is that of bride to the spirit of man. However, the meaning of the eternal order had been destroyed and hence the degradation of the essential union between man and woman necessarily followed upon the disintegration of the whole fabric of spiritual life. Organization replaced the vital interchange of powers, the bond of conformity to agreements superseded the natural bond that accords with God's will, and negotiation stood in the stead of mystery. The profound sense of being with one another became the workaday fact of being next to one another, where it had not already degenerated into being against one another.

The period of the rising feminist movement went parallel with the adoption of the nonsensical expression "struggle of the sexes". To make the movement responsible for this would be a profound inaccuracy as well as an injustice. Through it, however, even where such a battle was not sought and never took place, a danger zone was formed that is the feminine counterpart of the present-day leagues of men.[7]

And yet, the real and deepest danger to woman did not lie along this line of refusal, but in the opposite direction. The veil is not only the symbol of the bride of man, but also of the Bride of Christ. We have observed that the woman of the period in question was visible but not fundamentally effective. This means that even in becoming visible she must yet remain the representative of invisible powers. Léon Bloy's words "the holier a woman, the more she is a woman" are valid also in reverse, for the truly feminine role in every situation is irretrievably bound to her religious character.

The sublime and almost terrifying analogy that the Church uses at a marriage ceremony, the comparison to the union between Christ and the Church, has the profound purpose of impressing the woman with the truth that the bride of man should also be the bride of Christ and belongs to God. This alone gives to St. Paul's words that woman should be subject to man their deepest meaning. It is because he exacts this submission in a religious sense, that the inner freedom of the woman in her surrender becomes assured. The consciousness of belonging to God should protect her from herself; for her peril does not lie only in a refused surrender, but also in an exaggerated one. The mystery of charity,

---

[7] Whenever referring to leagues of men the author always has in mind certain groups that attracted attention in Germany during both world wars.—TRANS.

as we have indicated, can also degenerate. When her union with God has relaxed or dissolved, there is danger of woman's exaggerated surrender to man. It is then that her relationship to man absorbs also that which belongs to God. Such a relationship brings with it the same barrenness, the same absence of an ultimate horizon that we have recognized as deadly in a culture that is purely worldly. This latter type reflects only the degeneration of the mystery of charity. Along the entire line of our reasoning, the truth that most vitally concerns our times is that without eternal loyalties we lose not only eternity, but this life as well.

For the woman of the recent past this is to say that the quality that we are inclined to characterize as masculinity in the woman frequently reveals itself upon closer scrutiny as unrestrained femininity. There exists also a certain type of feminine humility that betrays the man and delivers him to his own pride. The so-called masculine woman represents only a variety of womanhood no longer devoted to man according to the spirit of the divine order. This order, which applies in all places and in every situation where man and woman meet, constitutes the mystery of charity in its profound interchange of giving and taking. Where the woman who no longer gives herself according to this divine order ends, the woman who either refuses herself or becomes the slave of man begins.

If we compare the so-called masculine woman with the heroines of the novels of the same period, we can easily discern their similarity. Even the woman of that time who persevered in the family frequently demonstrates the same type. As she lost herself to the man to the point of satiety and disgust, in the world of sense and emotion, so also along spiritual lines she surrendered herself unreservedly and with a lack of restraint that equaled a betrayal of the mystery of charity and a betrayal as well of her own inherent powers. She tried to share man's intellectual world and sank to the level merely of his methods. In the social world she sought for space to develop her deepest potentialities and allowed herself instead to be inserted as a link in his apparatus. In a doubly fatal way she succumbed as woman to the very one-sidedness, to the mistakes and the dangers upon which the man of the period had sickened. The error lay not so much in the objectives of the feminist movement and in the situations it created as in the character of the epoch, which, in its spiritual life, no longer knew its obligations or the direction of its final goal.

This at once indicates the result. A glance at the contemporary literature again points the way. The novels usually end with disconsolate uniformity in the breaking up of love and marriage. The woman who destroys love and marriage parallels the man who by infidelity and divorce rejects his wife. In succumbing to man, woman no longer surrenders; she throws herself away. She has nothing more to give, she is no longer man's other half. As woman she ceases to be, and the balance of life, its polarity, has been destroyed thereby. In clinging exclusively to the pole to which she does not properly belong, she loses the one that is her own; the mystery of charity with its profound reciprocity becomes extinguished, and the fruitfulness of the relationship ends. The exclusion of woman from man's spiritual activity entails results the same as those following upon the collapse of marriage.

By recognizing these facts, a correct attitude toward the present becomes possible. It is evident that at this point the past epoch reaches over into ours, with this difference, that the present accomplishes in an obvious and a conscious manner what the past has done unknowingly. In reality woman had lost her power as a symbol while she was still believed to be retaining it. A culture that in its last analysis is no longer turned toward God in reverence and with a sense of responsibility has, if viewed according to a deeper insight, also foregone the presence of woman. The woman, however, who recklessly and unconditionally allows herself to become part of such a culture, basically affirms only her own exclusion. Her presence is nothing more than a pretense.

We have said before that the mere situation in the past epoch was not decisive, neither is it decisive today. The recent deliberate attempt on the part of some of the leading countries of Europe to crowd woman out of cultural life has not in the least altered her conditions in things of the spirit. It is only the semblance of her presence that is destroyed. No further possibility exists, therefore, of establishing the full weight of the other half of reality than actually to be this other half and to recall the primal powers and the original role of womanliness. This is of extraordinary advantage to the woman. In her present situation there may, however, be danger of a renewed decision in favor of the errant way of the past, that woman may succumb to man, not as formerly, but in the opposite direction.

It is not the man but the woman who must save the endangered feminine image; she must rescue it in its threefold revelation as established by eternal decrees, for the totality of man and woman corresponds also to a totality of womanhood. The other half of being does not, as the present day would have it, include only the partial image of woman, that of the mother; it comprises likewise that of the virgin and the bride. The bride, who in the eyes of man represents both virgin and mother, expresses at the same time the totality of the womanly image.

To this totality of the image a totality of task conforms. The bride is not only the companion of man's life, but also of his spirit. She who is genuinely woman will never concern herself with only a part of man and his world; but as she desires his whole self, so she wishes to share the full extent of his life. Only by this complete participation can she be that which God has destined her to be, the other half of existence. Although of late the situation as such, of woman with regard to man, may not have been decisive, her position at his side is nevertheless of greatest and most universal significance.

Every fruitful criticism naturally presupposes an element of affirmation. Just as the past epoch has produced men and women of great spiritual stature who in personal adherence to God ranged far beyond their times, so likewise amid all the blunders and failures of the period there were stimuli and driving forces that led directly to God. As in the motivation of the feminist movement, so also in its striving toward sources, lay the inalienable truth that the past epoch has opened to woman spiritual fountainheads that should never again fail her; for they stream forth not only toward the professions, but toward the vocation of woman. But it is neither the self-will of man nor the willfulness of woman that is able to determine what the womanly vocation really is. Here St. Augustine's magnificent utterance applies: "Love God and do what you will." For the woman who in her union with God maintains the attitude of the fiat, that is, "Be it done unto me", one might give this thought a new interpretation and yet preserve the essential tendency by saying: Be truly a woman and do what you will.

It means but to put the seal upon these words to revert once more to the great women of the Ottonian period, when culture, at least in its bearing upon the individual woman, was at its peak, and the freedom of her participation in it accorded with the religious foundation of an entire epoch.

From this historical retrospect the way into the future grows clear. It agrees with what Berdyaev has in mind when, in his book *The New Middle Ages*, he alludes to the "extremely significant role of woman" and her "important part in the religious awakening of our times". "For the coming historic epoch," he continues,

> the growing significance of woman has nothing in common with a continuation of the modern movement for the emancipation of women which seeks to place woman on an equality with man and would lead her along masculine ways. That was an antihierarchic, a levelling movement.... It is not the emancipated woman, placed upon an equal footing with man; but it is the eternal womanly, that in the approaching historical period will increase in significance.

The greater significance that Berdyaev predicts for woman, the new significance to which these pages also allude, is therefore one that is distinctly different from the meaning of woman in the past. It would imply that the reflection of the womanly quality become visible again in the countenance of creative man. It is a question of restoring the mystery of charity as a divine order would have it. Here alone man and woman can meet one another creatively. This new significance concerns the reestablishment of a totality of being, mirrored in the culture of the period, the reestablishment of its abundance and its renewal or, in case of failure, its final ruin.

The destruction of the totality of being, which means to place separate parts instead of the whole into an absolute position, always and irrefutably means the ruination of the parts as well as of the whole. We have just seen that the betrayal of the mystery of charity is always a dual one. Woman apart from her character as symbol means woman separated from the religious quality, the "Be it done unto me." This results from the arrogance of the self-assertive man, but it may also be the consequence of woman's denial of her symbol.

Today both these perils have grown to colossal proportions. Let us not deceive ourselves. A culture that consistently refuses to accept God as its supreme law and objective must at the last accept him as its judgment and its end. All eternity has this twofold character in that it represents either the religious fullness of time or the fulfilling of time in its apocalyptic meaning, for the Apocalypse is the final form in which a dying culture indicates that which lies beyond its reaches.

The final Apocalypse of St. John's Revelation is preceded by apocalypses of separate cultural cycles, and here we can speak only of one of these. We should not envision its coming as in the lightning splendor of some transcendent tempest of angels. It is only the announcement of the "latter days" that is of visible magnitude, for their herald still stands under an eternal mandate that makes his prophetic vision possible. If the fulfillment of the prophecies were to strike our own cultural cycle, it would portray but a perishing multitude in a general destruction of monstrous proportions. An inner view, however, would reveal only the complete pettiness of a miserable annihilation.

The world of the Horsemen of the Apocalypse is not the kind of war that might be a man's heroic destiny, nor is it famine as failure on the part of nature, or disease and death as the discharging of elemental forces. Rather, it may be the work that results from mercenary principles that involve no sense of responsibility, or from a spirit of scholarship grown godless. We know today that these two evils are capable of annihilating entire harvests and poisoning a whole people. The woman in time, however, who will be the woman of those latter days is not the great whore of Babel of whom St. John tells, not the demoniacal temptress of recreant kings, but she will be the everyday little feminine creature who has leaped out of God's order, who, as a bearer of her eternal symbol, has ceased to be.

The absence of one part of reality, as we have intimated before, always produces unsteadiness in the image of the remaining part. Fundamentally, the world of the Four Horsemen is the world without woman. It is not indeed the man's world; for it is a world in which, for him also, the spirit of the Fiat mihi, "Be it done unto me", no longer exists, where there is no cooperation of the creature with God. It is the world without God, the world that, conditioned to the human being alone, assumes a destructive character. A culture that has become incapable of life dies no natural death; it strangles. With the invasion of the Four Horsemen the tragic course of a culture that has grown one-sided from both the immanent and the transcendental point of view continues with inexorable conclusiveness. The disintegration of the outer structure of the world but completes the destruction of its foundations.

The scales are still trembling. The profound consolation that woman can give to mankind today is her faith in the immeasurable efficacy also of forces that are hidden, the unshakable certainty that not only a visible but also an invisible pillar supports the world. When all the earthly potencies shall have exhausted themselves in vain, and this in the present distress of the world is nearly the case, then, even for a humanity largely grown godless, the hour of the other world will strike again. But the divine creative power will break forth from heaven to renew the face of the earth, only if the earth itself responds again with the religious force, with the readiness of the "Be it done unto me."

The hour of God's help is always mankind's religious hour, the hour of the woman, the hour of the creature's cooperation with the Creator. God grant that woman may not miss her approaching hour! On the agitating way between heaven and hell along which humanity is traveling today, the same guides to whom Dante long ago entrusted himself are needed. The poet and seer unfolds the vision of all the abysses and steps of purgation in the world of being; but he finds the way to Paradise only when he meets the loving woman whose eyes rest in God. The greatest poem of all times is both the most supernaturally sublime pronouncement and the eternally valid proof of the creative meaning of the mystery of charity.

TIMELESS WOMAN

A time like ours, that values the fact that it has in a sense rediscovered the mother in order to base upon her alone a new right belonging to woman, must come to understand clearly that with this discovery it has assumed a new and serious obligation to penetrate to the mothers themselves, to question them, as it were, concerning the essential character of motherhood. This demand of our time, made with such extraordinary emphasis, demonstrates primarily and above all that motherhood for the woman of today is no longer, as it was in former times, a matter of course. With this we must naturally admit also the possibility of misunderstanding true motherliness.

This danger is in fact quite evident. It is only the city dweller spending his weekends in the country who goes into raptures about nature; the farmer breathes in it. It is only the uncreative critic who is given to much talking about art. For the artist himself, his art is speech sufficient. It is only a motherless time that cries out for a mother, and a deeply unmotherly age that can point to the mother as a demand of the time, for it is precisely the mother who is timeless, the same in all epochs and among all peoples.

In her ageless form the differing destinies of queen and beggar woman lose their contrast. The distinguishing characteristics of nations and the disparities between primitive and highly developed levels of culture vanish in her presence. Motherhood can never become for woman the special assignment of a certain time; it is her task, simply and utterly. The mother as such does not bear the individualizing marks of the person, nor does she carry the stamp of an epoch. With her every temporal program ends, since time itself has no power over her. Under the form of virgin she stands solitary in the face of time; as bride she shares time with the man who lives in it; as mother she conquers time.

On earth the mother is the image of endlessness; centuries pass over her joy and her sorrow and leave no trace behind. She is ever the same, the boundless abundance, the silence, the immutability of life itself, in its power of conceiving, of bearing, of bringing forth. In this she is comparable only to the fruitful womb of the earth, which likewise we cannot urge, except within limits, to pour its blessings upon us, for in all the things that concern essential and original life, man's power of will and action never extends further than the foreground.

> Mysterious, even in the light of day
> Nature never will permit
> That her veil be torn away.

The motif that is basic to all that comes to pass through woman is in the highest measure fundamental also to woman's function of giving birth. The veil that the bride wears on her wedding day is not only the symbol of her inviolate virginity; it is symbolic also of the marriage upon which she is to enter. The same veil that conceals the bride enfolds also the cradle of her child. This is the profound meaning of the beautiful custom of carrying the child to baptism under the mother's bridal veil. Conception and birth are the hour and the mystery of life, which means that they are the hour and the mystery of woman.

It is this trait of mystery that Ruth Schaumann[8] points out in her letter *Chelion To Cletus* when she writes: "True women are quiet and desire quiet. . . . Show me the woman who writes about that which concerns her intimately. . . . If it did concern her she would be silent; for here silence is life; speech, death. . . . The mystery is always the fruitful thing; but disclosure is the end." Here Ruth Schaumann touches upon something more than the breaking in of our own time upon the woman who is timeless. If we glance simultaneously over the past decades, it becomes evident that the stirring cry for the mother reverberating through the present age expresses not so much the impact of the times upon the realm of the timeless woman, as it does the terror of the times at this invasion. Its portentous beginnings lie in the past. Not only do the public speeches and discussions of the last epoch about "The Right of Motherhood" and "The Cry for the Child" signify the inner peril to marriage and motherhood, but they actually constitute this menace. They do it even where they have been inspired by the best of intentions, and the tragedy of it is that this is exactly where they prove how total was the lack of understanding for the specific domain of the maternal woman, nay, of woman herself.

When viewed from this angle, novels and dramas of the period that were based on married life appear in a highly doubtful light. Obviously marriage, like every great, universally human theme, must be available as subject matter of genuine art, but art likewise must respect the boundaries of the silence that belongs to the inward reality of things. This does not mean, as the past epoch objected, to limit art in its creative functioning, but it does mean that art also

[8]Ruth Schaumann: Distinguished German Catholic poet and artist.

must follow the only possible way of drawing close to the heart of things. Unhappiness in marriages, taken both as a whole and individually, can be remedied only by having regard for this necessary inner domain, and the artist also must recognize it, if he is to portray conditions creatively.

It is true that both these points of view were extremely difficult for a time like the past epoch to accept, accustomed as it was always to focus its hopes only upon that which it undertook, carried on, and discussed with an activity that was visible far and wide. In this respect our own time is still largely in alignment with the past. This is particularly evident in the call for the mother that echoes throughout its reaches. This appeal, although altogether justified, nevertheless denotes a fundamental and an absolute helplessness. As we intimated above, in all the things that concern essential and original life, the volitional and the active powers of man never penetrate beyond the foreground. Our times have recognized correctly the dangers to motherhood that come from the self-love and degeneration of woman. In most cases the elemental mother nature that is in her would prevail; it would likewise be able to tear the fetters imposed upon her by economic necessity, were it not that nature itself is in chains.

A fettering of the natural forces that threaten man always means a restriction also of the natural potentials of man. We must make it clear to ourselves that even the most beneficial form, such as modern medicine and hygiene, in which the invasion of the times into the domain of timeless woman expresses itself, is after all an invasion and constitutes the positive side of an enormous technical transformation of all the natural functions of motherhood. The advantage that the future mother derives from the clinic, for her own health and that of her child, is purchased at the expense of tearing

away the mystery of birth not only from the shared experience of the family, which constitutes the original and natural shelter for the mystery, but also from the awesomeness
of the primal powers that are its carriers.

The reverence for nature, which the demand of today
for the natural destiny of woman presupposes, depends necessarily upon the degree to which nature may still be regarded
as absolute mistress. The disappearance of respect for the
sovereignty of nature becomes understandable at once as an
attending circumstance of man's technical mastery of nature,
if we become aware not only of the positive application of
present-day scientific methods but also of their negative
aspects. The increased possibility of preserving the life of
the child is paralleled by the equally increased possibility of
preventing or even removing the child. Consequently, today
we no longer see all around us the woman who is in reality
subservient to the great, unsearchable forces of nature and
ministers to them with reverence. In her place we have the
woman whose timeless character is protected yet hard pressed
on all sides by the forces of time—ensured, but also infringed
upon by them. We must have all this in mind if we would
grasp the startling import of the call of today for the mother.

For this reason the demand that we revert to the mother
in her essential character cannot by any means be regarded
as identical with the questioning of the individual mother
of the present. It does, however, concern the disclosure of
evidences beyond the personal, of the mother quality in its
innermost nature; thus rendering visible, above all temporal
limitations, the form of the timeless woman. Herewith we
shall find ourselves once more upon the terrain of great
art.

At once something remarkable becomes evident. For the
image of the mother, supremely great art for the most part

directs us to that which it conceals. Great drama, especially, withholds almost all information regarding the mother. In *King Lear* Shakespeare has portrayed the tragedy of the father; that of the mother is missing. We have only the cry of Constance in *King John*; and in *Coriolanus* the two mothers merely stand in contrast to the masculine protagonist. The old mother demonstrates the truth that a mother desires to act and to receive honor only through her son, but the young mother is addressed as "My lovely Silence". Does the moving beauty of this wondrous title signify that art also is in agreement with what Ruth Schaumann says about the individual woman when she writes: "If it concerned her she would be silent"?

Does this silence mean, in its deeper sense, that art also knows about the mother? Much could be said for this insofar as great dramatic art is concerned. Every genuine drama revolves around the hour of heroism. Woman's heroic hour, unlike that of man, is not the revelation of an action that is visible at long range; it fulfills itself rather in deepest retirement. As woman recedes from the public gaze, so she withdraws herself from being dramatized. But there is, in addition, a further tendency. Dramatic art does not catch fire only from heroic action, but also from the single figure, from its own special law and development. The mother, however, is not a single figure, and she has no law of her own. Her law is the child, and whatever is centered elsewhere is more or less impersonal to her.

The mother is the timeless woman, for she is immutable. Her love does not develop, for the immutable does not increase. From the first moment it is there. Mother love cannot be augmented, since this would imply that once it was less great. Development does not determine the various periods of a mother's life, but these periods are like the lapse of the seasons. Spring and autumn are not developments; they are the parts of an unending cycle.

As at the hour of birth the mother stakes her life without reserve for the child, so after its birth her life no longer belongs to herself, but to the child. The timeless woman is she who has become engulfed in the stream of the generations; the maternal woman is the one who has submerged herself in the child. Of her Friedrich Hebbel writes:

> She has borne a child
> To loftiest joy and deepest grief,
> And now she is completely lost
> In its mute loveliness.

The natural and immeasurable love that streams from the mother, and as it were constitutes the shelter within which the child grows to its stature as a person, means for the mother surrender and sacrifice to the point of placing her own stature and her own personality in jeopardy. This in turn must be interpreted in a thoroughly heroic and not at all in a pathetic sense. As the heroic hour of birth fulfills itself behind the curtain, so the heroism of the mother's life continues in profound simplicity. The nursery replaces the room of her heavy hour, while she who has passed life on into endlessness fulfills her own living in an unending succession of little and infinitesimal cares. As the mother's heroism is linked with silence, so also it is bound to that which is average and everyday.

This means that the art form to which the mother is accessible is not the drama, the form of powerful destinies and personalities, but rather the novel, which is the homely art of the everyday. Even as a literary form the novel represents the modest, average qualities that associate themselves with the type of destiny and heroism that belong to the mother. Through its relationship with daily and trivial events, the novel is in a special manner qualified to unfold lovingly the unending trifles that represent a mother's life.

Her really great lines, however, her universal quality—the unpsychological, the immutable, the elemental in her, the part that is so closely bound to nature, in short, timeless woman—is not to be found in the time-conditioned art of the novel, but rather in the naïve art of folklore. All that estranges the mother from the drama opens the way to her for the saga and the fairy tale, which do not concern themselves with individual but with typical forms. The mother of the fairy tale is always the same mother. It is especially when she is dead that the fairy tale portrays the unchangeable quality of her love, her inseparability from her child.

Fundamentally, no fairy tale assumes that a mother could die, for death has no power over love or over the immutable. The dead mother of the fairy tale returns at night and rocks her children or permits nature lovingly to take her place. The mother arms reach out for the orphaned child in the branches of the little tree that has sprung from her grave, and mother hands shower it with gifts. The Breton saga tells of the Berceuse, the death-woman who whispers into the ears of the dying mariners of sinking ships lullabies that she had heard their mothers sing. Here the mother of folklore touches upon the deep accord between birth and death.

As nature takes the place of the mother, so the mother represents nature. Sometimes she is felt to be entirely a creature of nature, as in the story of the lovely Melusine. From the profound naturalness with which the fairy tale experiences the mother comes also its prejudice against the stepmother. Only the genuine mother can be the right one;

hence the stepmother, as not appointed by nature, is always evil. The blood relative, however, the sister of the children of the fairy tale, takes the place of the mother who has died, as she does in the story of the *Seven Ravens* and in *Little Brother and Little Sister*. As in the fairy tale, so in the folk song the essential mother impulse emerges strongly. The lullaby portrays it by its very form. Through the lips of the mother, expressing all her tenderness and all her love, it sings to the child alone.

As the mother is not a subject for the drama, neither is she the real theme for sculptural art. That which personality means to drama, form means to sculpture. Personality is a solitary thing and form possesses contour. The form of the mother is not sharply outlined, but flows into the form of the child. As in literature it is the novel, the song, the fairy tale, so painting as the art not of form, but of color, is the medium particularly destined to present the mother and child. It is no mere accident that these figures are entirely absent from Greek art. So pictorial a subject matter was naturally resistant to the highly developed sculptural feeling of classical antiquity. It is only Christianity that carries the form of mother and child into sculpture, but in its sacred character. The Madonna is the bearer of the Divine, the torch, as it were, that carries the Light of the world. She is the pedestal of the Child, not a purpose in herself.

Nor does Christian art work out the form of the mother independently; but it places her in a subordinate position, the more to reveal in her quiet posture the enchanting quality of motherhood. The loveliness of the Madonna's face is but the symbol of this inner beauty. Thus the impossibility for art to fashion her as standing alone follows from the very essence of the mother's nature, and the artist can do it only in separating the mother from the child. The genuine mother figure of sculpture is therefore the Sorrowful Mother, the Mother under the Cross of her Son. That which breaks the mother to the very depths of her nature makes her possible as a subject for plastic art. For this reason also, ancient sculpture, while ignorant of the image of mother and child, still knows the figure of Niobe.

This again throws light upon the relationship between dramatic art and the mother. Her figure, detached from that of the child, is not only that of the mother of a dead son, but it may also be that of a degenerate mother. Once more sculpture and drama stand under the same law. The rending of the mother from the child makes her an independent figure and therefore capable of dramatic treatment. Of this Medea is the most outstanding example. The Jocasta of *King Oedipus* and the Queen in *Hamlet* also belong to this category. In both these characters degeneration appears as resulting from the predominance of the erotic over the maternal quality. This group includes also Krimhild of the *Nibelungenlied*, dramatically conceived, although in epic form. She is probably the most unmotherly figure in all literature. In the bloody revenge for the death of her husband she sacrifices not only her brothers, but even her own child. With gruesome yet poetic magnificence, the most powerful figure in German literature testifies that not every woman who has a child is a mother.

Here, under the guidance of literature, we stumble upon the decisive question. Precisely in our own time, which has desired to see woman exclusively in the mother, the problem of woman that we believed to have solved in terms of the mother presents itself again in the mother herself. Every age at the final issue finds woman's problem in the very place where it has sought its solution. The answer that art as the timeless resort of our period gives is that the mother for whom the human race of today is calling with such deep yearning cannot be only the woman who has a child. "To go down to the mothers", as Goethe expressed it in *Faust*, means to penetrate more profoundly than merely to the physical mother; it means to search for the mother in the mother herself. In accord with this idea, the great Nordic writer Sigrid Undset has something to say in her novel *Ida Elisabeth*.

The opening pages of the book sound the theme at once, when a young girl says: "When we see how egotistic many people become through family ties, we can readily imagine that God would, if only for the sake of compensation, select a few and allow them to be all things to all." Ida Elisabeth, the heroine of the story, who is entirely disposed toward motherhood in its natural sense, abruptly rejects this idea of being all things to all. She has the misfortune of being married to a man of infantile character and is obliged to work not only for his support, but also for that of his parents, brothers, and sisters.

"Women", she says, "who have the feeling that they are here to bear children, hate and despise it when grown men come and force them to be as mothers also to them." Ida Elisabeth separates from her husband in order to provide a better livelihood for her two little sons, to whom alone she feels bound by a mother's duty. Only now does the actual question of her maternal life arise. In her children she drags the unsolved problem of her marriage along with her. From the consideration of her children begins her coming to an understanding with a man of full stature whom she loves and wishes to marry. The children carry the heritage of their immature father. As in the first marriage the inferiority of her husband, so now the superior endowment of the man she loves becomes the problem of her destiny. The question is not whether, by a second marriage, she can unite husband and children, but whether or not she will be able to bring into accord this man of character and the children who are marked with the stamp of their inadequate father. In short, the problem of the book is: Does this motherly woman owe herself to the strong man or to the weakling?

From this self-questioning slowly a decision rises from the heart of Ida Elisabeth. It is not the need to sacrifice for her children's sake her betrothal to the man she loves, for one of the finest features of the novel, some of its most ingenious artistry, lies in the avoidance of the idea of sacrifice. Ida Elisabeth's decision results without any reflection and is formed beyond her own thinking; it emerges from the depths of her maternal nature. The decision is nevertheless absolute and carries all its consequences within itself. This becomes evident when again she meets her husband, who in the meantime had become seriously ill. She no longer refuses herself to him and his family. The mother in her has conquered throughout; the decision is not in favor of the man who is strong, but of those who are weak.

To be a mother, to feel maternally, means to turn especially to the helpless, to incline lovingly and helpfully to every small and weak thing upon the earth. Therefore the principle of motherhood is a dual one; it attaches itself not only to the birth of the child, but to the fostering and protecting of that which has been born. To become a mother physically means but the first breaking forth of the powers of maternity; it is only the first moving symbol of something that is much more universal. It is her own children who lead Ida Elisabeth to the realization that the maternal woman cannot remain the mother only of her own children.

Not alone is the child born through the mother, but the mother also is born through the child. "It is the children who awaken us, who say: how hard you are; become gentle!" Ruth Schaumann writes in her book entitled *Yves*. The child that at its birth breaks through its mother's womb breaks through her heart also, opening it to all that is small and weak.

As the face of the Madonna of the Mantle in a wayside shrine emerges through the darkness of the forest, so in Sigrid Undset's novel, amid a thicket of problems that human beings fashion, the thought arises that a mother is really the mother of all. In Ida Elisabeth's husband and his family an extreme case is described, but that which applies to them, at the final issue, applies everywhere and always. The world has need of the maternal woman; it is, for the most part, a poor and helpless child. As man comes feebly into the world, so in profound weakness he departs from it, and the mother who wraps the child in its infant clothes has the merciful hand of the woman who supports the aged and wipes the sweat from the brows of the dying. Between birth and death lies not only the achievement of the successful, but the unending weariness of the way, the continuous monotony, all that belongs to the needs of the body and of life.

The maternal woman is appointed the quiet stewardess of this inexhaustible inheritance of necessity and distress. Under this aspect of mother, woman does not represent, as she does as bride, the one half of reality. Her part is probably much more than half. People know why the man calls his wife "Mother". In doing so he does not address only the mother of his children, but the mother of everyone, which means, above all, the mother of her own husband.

It is the mother who prepares his meals, sets his table, mends his clothes, bears his inadequacies, his anxieties, his difficult hours. "The heart of her husband trusteth in her and he shall have no need of spoils" [Prov 31:11], says the

Bible in praise of the valiant woman. "And she hath risen
in the night and given a prey to her household" [Prov 31:15].
The mother of the man is the mother of all his household.
This mother, too, is always the same. Like the mother of
the child she can be compared only to the bountiful earth
that gives and bears and gives and bears again; and finally
by very reason of this humble earthliness she overcomes the
bond of earth. It is the maternal woman, overwhelmed as
she is by the needs of every day, who is the great conqueror of the every day. Daily she controls it anew by making it bearable, and her victory is greatest when least
observed.

The man who in the intellectual field exerts himself to
overcome materialistic influences can succeed only when
the maternal woman actually clears them away. The unpre-
tentiousness of this daily victory, its complete obscurity, is
the real and innermost glory of the timeless woman, comparable only to that of the unknown soldier of World War I.
He is the son of the unknown woman.

In addition to the physical needs of life come the heavy
trials that burden the mind and spirit of human beings, the
enormous weight of sorrow and trial, of inadequacy and
guilt of all kinds that, in the majority of cases, cannot be
removed and must simply be borne. As the motherly woman
feeds the hungry, so also does she console the afflicted. The
weak and the guilty, the neglected and the persecuted, even
the justly punished, all those whom a judicial world no longer wishes to support and protect, find their ultimate rights
vindicated in the consolation and the compassion that the
maternal woman gives. For her the words of Antigone will
always be valid: "Not to hate, but to love with you, am I
here." This does not mean to set up weakness as against
strength. Quite the contrary. The Bible does not sing the

praise of the weak woman, but of the strong one, in the words of the Book of Proverbs: "The law of clemency is on her tongue" [31:26]. It is patience that is strength in highest potency.

To the privileges of the maternal woman belongs the quiet, extremely important function of knowing how to wait and be silent, the ability sometimes to overlook, spare, and cover up a weakness. As a work of mercy this is no lesser charity than clothing the naked. It belongs to the ominous errors of the world, to the fundamental reason of its lack of peace, to believe that it must always uncover and condemn all that is wrong. Every wise and kindly mother knows that sometimes it is right to do exactly the opposite.

The quotation from the Bible cited above, "The law of clemency is on her tongue", follows the words "She hath opened her mouth to wisdom." This wisdom is often but a pleasantry or a friendly word. In this, too, the woman is veiled. Her wisdom does not manifest itself as something great, but as an insignificant thing, and therein lies its greatness. This does not mean to consign the masterly and judicial wisdom of the man to a secondary place, but it does signify the admission that it is but one side of the truth. To the very man who would contest this characteristic of the maternal woman, the world would become unbearable if she were to lose this quality. Even the man who grudgingly or without understanding submits to this simple wisdom draws from it the strength that makes life possible for him. It is often the last resource of patience, kindness, and forbearance, without which all existence, be it of the individual or of nations, is in danger of becoming a hell. This is the general if not the fully Christian sense of the lovely legend of St. Elizabeth's miracle of roses. It is the simple legend of a woman's motherliness.

Just as the miracle of roses continues to repeat itself, so also does the protest of the landgrave, her husband. Woman's universal motherhood, its absolute relationship to the small and weak, necessarily includes the question of the meaning or the justification of the small and weak things of the world. Man is willing to acknowledge them only under the form of something capable of growth. Hereupon we confront the second problem in the novel *Ida Elisabeth*, the problem that lies in the distinction between two worlds, that of the man and that of the maternal woman. The following quotation introduces the subject: "Must we not judge the good that is in human beings, as we would a vein of ore that causes us to ask whether or not it is rich enough to warrant the labor spent upon it?"

Doubtless, Ida Elisabeth's husband belongs to those who are not worth the effort, one whom we can designate only as a failure. This is to define a condition as unalterable; it means that here the laws of growth or progress no longer have a place. But does it end the duty of being motherly? With this question the novel enters upon its concluding stage. Plainly it is a matter of the value or the worthlessness of the person as such. At this point the path of the mother and that of the virgin intersect and suddenly we are standing again at the margin of the mystery of all that is imperfect and unfulfilled.

But now, in Sigrid Undset's novel, a wonderful thing happens. The motherly woman, the very one whom our times have placed over against the unfruitful, the solitary woman, embraces that which has remained fruitless, the incomplete thing, that which, according to earthly standards, is a misfit. The deathbed of Ida Elisabeth's failure of a husband brings the message:

Everything by which human beings make something of their lives: love, work, responsibility, these things were and continue

to be sufficiently great, now and always; but today a light
or a darkness rests upon them, so that the forms that dif-
ferentiate one human life from another, have vanished. "Is
it God," Ida Elisabeth asks, "in whose hands all the irrec-
oncilable contrasts lie?" And now the face of the deadman
gives the answer, "this radiant, terrifying, this almost triumphant final countenance."

Was its inconceivable beauty the image of that which
should have been? Was it the sublimity of the thought that
the Creator encloses even into the work that has apparently
been a failure? Was this beauty the token that the incomprehensible would not always remain incomprehensible? The
final evaluation of the human being is not incumbent upon
man, but belongs to God. According to Sigrid Undset's novel,
it is not man in his judgments, but woman in her motherliness, who, in the face of death, will stand confirmed
before God.

One dare not forget, however, that in temporal affairs
Sigrid Undset's novel permits the man's evaluation to stand
in its full strength; it stands even for the maternal woman.
She who must take care of the one who has failed, and
must do it with unappraising, unquestioning patience, shares
fully in the responsibility for the failure. She is like the wife
who, as the bride of man's spirit, carries with him the responsibility for his cultural work, and the wife who as future
mother participates in the responsibility for the child.

It must be clearly understood, however, that in the appraisal
that this responsibility presupposes we are regarding only
one side of the matter. Man must maintain the evaluation
of this world if he wants to fulfill his mission in its regard.
He can therefore admit weakness only in that which is in
process of becoming something, not in that which already
is established as it is. The unconditional motherliness of the

woman, on the other hand, that embraces the weakness even in that which is, stands close to the borders of the world beyond. Only in this light does the appraisal of man have the obligation of acknowledging the maternal world. The miracle of St. Elizabeth's roses signifies the sanction of earthly compassion by eternal mercy.

This gives not only the service of the motherly woman in behalf of weakness but weakness itself its metaphysical meaning. Here we come upon the region where the vein of inferior ore nevertheless becomes worthwhile. Man's limitations are always God's port of entry. The little, the weak, the insufficient ones of the earth are here to show human beings the way to eternal mercy. They represent human and earthly insufficiency in its gentlest, most appealing form; its more grievous, more agonizing aspect appears as sin and guilt. Therefore the weak and little ones of the earth not only possess the Kingdom of heaven, as the Gospel tells, but they proclaim it by opening the way to it.

In this mission, she who protects and cares for them participates. The words of St. Paul, that the woman should win salvation by the bearing of children, find their completion in the blessing pronounced upon the merciful. If a ray from the happiness and the dignity of Mary's motherhood rests upon every maternal woman, a radiance also descends from the crown of the Mother of Mercy.

From this general concept of woman's motherly quality, the correct appreciation of spiritual motherhood follows. This too is a natural power of love, determined by the innate tendency of woman, even when it does not come through her own child. This is the motherliness of which the German fairy tale shows a premonition in the little sister spinning shirts for the brother ravens who are under a charm; it is the mother quality already present in the child and surviving in the older girl beyond the hope of physical motherhood. Since spiritual maternity is a natural tendency, its unfolding also is a thoroughly natural one. If we said before that physical motherhood is but the first breaking forth of the mother's powers, their most universal, most appealing aspect, this does not mean that a woman can attain to motherhood in this universal sense only through her own child. It is a remnant of the period of individualism to believe that everyone must experience everything.

The real mother sometimes represents the woman who possesses only spiritual maternity, just as in many instances the woman who is maternal only in a spiritual way must substitute for the woman who has a child, but is not in the true sense its mother. In the family it may for instance be the relative or godmother, in public life the guardian, who fills this position. It is not a matter of the destiny of the individual woman, but of her participation in the universal destiny of woman; it is that motherliness of every woman, untouched by external destinies, that counts. If Ruth Schaumann in her novel *Yves* says, "She does not know what a mother is; she has never given birth to a child", she refutes the statement in the same book through the character of Germaine, who is denied the joy of having children of her own, but who takes the strange child to her heart with a mother's *love*, while its own mother deserted it.

Occasionally the stepmother, whom the fairy tale uses so ill, belongs to the category of Germaine, the childless but motherly woman. In Anselm Feuerbach's faithful stepmother she finds herself vindicated. Nevertheless this does not place the fairy tale in the wrong. It knows the depth and the unique quality of the tie that unites mother and child, but it does not know all the possibilities of the maternal nature; it does not understand that the spiritual side of motherhood also is a part of nature. The legend, however, does justice to this other mother, and art has represented the Madonna of the childless woman and of the step-mother in Holbein's painting, where the Madonna does not carry the Infant Jesus, but the donor's sick child in her arms.

From this point of view woman's demand for a child of her own appears in a different light. It is not always inspired by the genuine mother quality. On the contrary, it some-times reveals a very feminine form of egoism which leaves but a phantom of the true mother. King Solomon did not allow himself to be deceived by this illusion. To his wis-dom it was the renunciation of the child that gave proof of the real mother. The past decades with their "Cry for the Child" and "Right of Motherhood" have given fatal help in setting up this phantom in place of the real mother.

As indicated before, there is no such thing as a woman's right to a child; there is only the right of the child to a mother. Ruth Schaumann's words "Only children make us gentle, for they say: 'How hard you are! Become gentle!'" retain their full significance not only with regard to a child not one's own, but also when there is question of those who may be said to represent the child, the helpless with their arms outstretched, and all those in general who need care and protection. For the woman who is maternal in the spiritual sense, this gives the correct insight into the ques-tion of vocation so far as women are concerned. For a woman to be a physician, a guardian, teacher, or nurse is therefore not a profession in the masculine sense of the word, but it is a form of spiritual motherhood.

The past epoch required a profession for the unmarried woman as a substitute for motherhood. The future, inspired by the concept of spiritual maternity, will call for it, but from the fulsome motherliness that is also in the single woman. The professions of women will consequently not be the substitute for a failing motherhood, but rather the working out of the never failing motherliness that is in every genuine woman.

The decisions whether women should engage in the various professions, and their choice of them, will depend upon the extent to which maternal activity can still be regarded as fruitful. A great number of professions without doubt admit of a purely masculine and a purely maternal interpretation, respectively. In this matter the apparently least feminine of professions, that of politics, is specially instructive. It is not by chance, but most intimately connected with the universal and the spiritual motherhood of woman, that when she was called to the throne to be an independent sovereign she was for the most part a good ruler, not in the purely masculine sense of the word, but a good queen, that is, the mother of her people. For this reason in Spain today the memory of the formerly ruling queen has survived the fall of dynasty and form of government. Not only does England remember Queen Bess, and Austria its great motherly empress Maria Theresa, but the Lombardy of today still recalls its Queen Theodolinde.

The woman on the throne is primarily the protectress of her people. The engrafting of the governing upon the maternal power does not, however, exclude the heroic impulse, which is indispensable to political life. Maria Theresa gives proof. Even as defender of her people the woman ruler does not lose her maternal quality. She will not lead wars of conquest, but she will defend her people as the lioness does her young. Only when she has betrayed her maternal character has woman in great political positions been a fatal influence—when, for instance, she plays the role of a Madame Pompadour.

The same applies to the average woman who enters political life. We need not necessarily picture her only as we have seen her in the recent past, for the woman who moves in diplomatic circles or travels abroad has an entirely natural political duty to fulfill, by which she may either help or harm her country. Although in humbler garb than that of queen, the woman in politics is in spirit a mother to her people. Only on this condition can her presence there be approved. No man can replace the voice of a mother; there is question only of how this voice may make its influence felt without distortion.

The recognition of the fact that there is no right on the part of the woman to a child, but only a right of the child to a mother, corresponds to the recognition of another fact that is pertinent to the present, namely, that there is in the world no woman's right, so called, to a profession or vocation, but the world has a child's right to the woman. If all indications are not deceiving, this right has assumed a highly intensified meaning during the past decades. The cry of today for the mother has its origin not only in desires aroused by problems of population and politics, but its undertone carries the weight of a spiritual longing. There is nothing that denotes the condition of the world today more profoundly and tragically than the complete absence of the maternal attitude of mind. It means the absence of the sustaining, the bearing, and therefore the fruit-yielding forces of life. The urge alone never suffices; hence we see the terrifying lack of blessing in so many efforts that are in themselves good and useful.

With these thoughts we have apparently abandoned the topic of timeless woman, but only apparently. In reality we are abandoning rather the consideration of time. The timeless woman is she who time cannot control, for to surmount time is of the essence of the mother quality. As the woman in giving birth carries life on into endlessness, so in her capacity of nurturing and sheltering life she injects into time an element of eternity.

In connection with her spiritual motherhood, woman's part in culture reveals itself once more. Under her aspect of mother she unquestionably becomes the one who protects and fosters cultural values. Unlike her role of wife, by which she supplies an essential half of the reality that enters into the cultural work of man, in her role of mother she takes this very work into her care. The one who receives, however, is for the most part the one who sustains. We have heard the valiant woman of the Bible praised as the keeper of her husband's goods. This care of the man's possessions woman transfers also to his intellectual sphere of life, and her role of receiving and sustaining endows her with an extraordinary significance for culture. Giving without receiving would fall into a void. It is not due only to the facts that woman often has more time and is more relaxed than man, that she is primarily the one who frequents the bookshop, the concert hall, and the theater, but it is associated with the spiritual destiny of her motherhood. Culture must not only be created; it must likewise be sustained, cherished, even loved like a child. It is but one side, and that the more exterior, of the fostering of culture if, as today, it is regarded and exercised largely as the concern of the State. Its fulfillment on the inward human side must come from the love and care that the individual gives.

Here once more the orbit of the spiritual crosses that of the physical mother. The mother who teaches her child its first words of the language that throughout life will remain its mother tongue, who sings to the child its first native songs and tells to it the fairy tales of its people, represents the first determining cultural factor, the earliest spiritual influence in the life of the child. This is of immeasurable importance not only for the child, but for culture. The Spanish proverb "The hand that rocks the cradle rules the world" means first of all that everyone who lives and labors is born of woman. Woman is the mother of the hero and of the saint; she is also the mother of the coward and the traitor. Surely when the antichrist is born, he will have many mothers. The deeper sense of this world-governing hand, however, consists in the fact that it will continue to lead the son invisibly throughout his later life and in its hidden way will work with him in the accomplishment of his task.

Woman's part as protectress of culture may also become that of its defender, similar to her position in the political world. She is by nature conservative, which, less pedantically expressed, means that she is incapable of betraying or destroying that which is endangered. This is an attitude which, in times of upheaval, may mount to an extraordinary significance. Times of upheaval easily succumb to the danger of surrendering not only outmoded but also timeless possessions. It is here that by reason of her spiritual motherliness woman is primarily called upon to establish a balance. The timeless woman is the keeper of the timeless possessions of her people.

On the other hand there is nothing that contributes so effectively to the downfall of culture as the decline of woman's spiritual motherhood. In this event the protectress of culture has become its squanderer. By comparison the pleasure-loving woman of recent times is relatively harmless. Herself in possession of the advantages of culture, fostering them almost to the point of worship without rendering them fruitful or sharing them with others, this type of woman is in a measure sister to the selfish mother who wants her child for herself alone. Such an attitude indicates a lack of reverence for the purposes of culture, although not as yet for culture in itself.

Along the same line by which a woman in descending from her womanliness loses the sense of motherhood, so also in declining from her cultural level she loses the sense for that which really requires care. She accordingly shows an inclination to become loud, strident, unsophisticated. This tendency is the form peculiar to woman when she loses her standards of cultural evaluation. There is a fine but extremely significant line from that which is originally unimportant, overlooked, misunderstood, or even opposed, leading to the very height of culture, that is, from out of its own time into timelessness. A glance at the history of great men and their lifework will demonstrate the agreement that exists largely between this line of thought and their destinies, indicating the more conclusively that the enduring does not and cannot depend upon the momentary. Of this the life stories of persons like Hebbel, Nietzsche, and Richard Wagner serve as examples. They are instances also of the cultural significance of the maternal woman. She who is timeless has relationship to that which is beyond time.

She is related, therefore, to that which is eternal, for at the final issue the import of all culture points to that which is beyond it. The role of the motherly woman as its protectress completes itself primarily in her role as the guardian of religious values and becomes thoroughly intelligible only through the position of the mother in the religious world.

In motherhood as nature has fashioned it, life and death rest beside one another. The stream of generations breaks forth out of eternity, and there also it empties itself. Endlessness is the earthly sister of eternity. The Berceuse of the

Breton saga, who whispers into the ears of perishing sailors the songs that she heard their mothers sing, finds a profound interpretation in the novel *Ida Elisabeth*, through the death of little Sölvi. In describing the feelings of the mother of the dying child, Sigrid Undset writes:

> It seemed to her as though she had lived through this before, when giving birth, at the moment when the child came forth from her and a wave from out of some titanic, endless sea washed over her, tearing something away. But when the wave rolled back again, a whimpering, quivering little being lay beside her, as though they both had been thrown upon the strand. The same breaker from out of an invisible eternity was now passing over her, and the wild, rending woe that she felt before in her body, was trifling in comparison with that which was tearing her today. The surf receded; but this time it had carried Sölvi away with it.

The surf that breaks forth out of eternity and rolls back to eternity opens the mother's womb as it were, at the moment of birth like a portal leading two ways. The life that comes out of an invisible eternity enters the visible world of time. From eternity to eternity, religiously expressed, means but one thing: from God to God.

With this concept we shall leave *Ida Elisabeth*. That this insight comes from a region beyond even the reality of woman's universal motherhood, and rises out of the essential nature of the mother herself, gives evidence of the imaginative power of this novel—above all, of its gripping finality. It is also the exposition, in creative form, of the theological tenet that nature constitutes the basis for grace, that grace functions everywhere not in contradiction, but in correspondence with and as a continuation of the ascending plane of nature. *Ida Elisabeth*, therefore, leads us only to the door of the Church where the figure of another woman awaits us: Sigrid Undset's *Kristin Lavransdatter.*

The significance of this tremendous novel that stands at the threshold of a time of spiritual upheaval that is still of incalculable proportions has lifted this upheaval on the part of woman into the general consciousness. The symptomatic meaning of such writing is that here a woman with all her powers, with all the forces of a full-blooded, unbroken womanliness and motherliness, is made to confront our epoch, uprooted as it is, insofar as the direction toward nature is concerned. This woman is at the same time the counterthrust against the religious rootlessness of the age. The first two volumes, *The Bridal Wreath* and *The Mistress of Husaby*, are filled with the storming naturalness of Nordic forces of blood and destiny; but the third volume has *The Cross* as subtitle. Along the way of Kristin's destiny we go through the entire development that emanates from the natural quality of a woman and a mother's life and flows into the character of the Christian mother. Kristin, which means "she who becomes a Christian", comes to the Church, but the Church approaches her through her nature, for it is precisely from the union between nature and the life of a mother that she fashions the points of contact with the religious destiny of woman and mother.

The Church also respects woman in her natural capacity of mother. The nuptial Mass is filled with the promise of the blessings of children: "May you see the children of your children!" In physical motherhood the Church beholds the original and primal destiny of woman and sees in her the mother of people and of nations. With magnificent vision, the prayers with which she supports her as she faces her difficult hour range far beyond individual life: "O may all peoples praise you! May the races be glad and rejoice, for the land is giving forth its fruit!" At the moment when the woman withdraws into the deepest concealment, the Church intones over her the great hymn of all peoples and uplifts her, mute with pain, into a glorification of God the Creator. In the consecration of a queen, the Church proclaims the same thought, while she anoints her below the heart where she is to carry the child.

The undelivered child in its mother's womb is in a two-fold sense undelivered. As the mother must bring it physically into the world, so the Church gives it supernatural life, for the Church also is a maternal concept, in the spiritual and religious sense. When she prays over the woman, who in suffering and in danger of death is about to bring a living child into the world, two mothers are face to face with one another. Life in itself, the unending recurrence of conception and birth, is not a final value. Ultimate value and meaning arise only from out of a higher life.

The Church has not given the mother the distinction of a special consecration such as the virgin and the bride receive. In relation to the consecration of a virgin or even to the sacrament of matrimony, the blessing given to the woman who is to become a mother, as well as the churching of the mother after the birth of the child, represents a blessing such as one might pronounce over a budding meadowland. The earthly birth is but the first step. This apparent undervaluing of the mother but accentuates her actual dignity, the extreme humility of nature in this complete surrender, not desiring to be more than simply nature, yet by this very attitude rising above itself into the meaning of the words of the *Magnificat*: "He hath exalted the humble."

Nature can be wild, but never willful; she may rear up with pain, but never with pride. Even in savagery, even in pain, nature fulfills the law of the Creator. The spirit,

however, must yield itself to him. The woman who, ready
to meet death, surrenders herself to the forces of nature in
order to give life to her child, by this very surrender, by
this complete submersion, portrays a part of the humble
quality that nature possesses. The mother, in giving earthly
life to the child, gives with it the prerequisite of redemption. Again, nature is the basis for grace.

With this theological principle the concept of the defense
of the child touches bedrock. The blessing and the curse
once pronounced upon woman echo as from an immeasurable distance. The prophecy that she shall bring forth
her children in pain and the promise of the Woman who
shall crush the serpent's head stand in closest relationship.
The significance of nature as the first step toward grace is
the presentation for supernatural birth, of the child that has
been born.

We have come to the place of the great sacrament that is
most intimately in accordance with maternal life. It is not
for the mother, however, but for the child. Baptism is the
child's second, its supernatural birth, and the bosom of the
Church that receives it is the mother bosom of its higher
life. For the earthly mother the gracious analogy with the
field that bears a blessing remains. This blessing rests upon
the field, but is meant primarily for the fruit, and the bread
that comes from the wheat is charged with high destiny.
Upon the altar it becomes the carrier of the Body of the
Lord. In the presence of the supernatural mother, the earthly
mother recedes. Because of the wish of the Church that
the child be baptized as soon as possible, the attendance of
the mother is in most instances impossible. This is deeply
symbolic. The mother gives evidence again that she is bound
by nature and, as such, is but the first step to the supernatural birth of the child. Therefore not she but the sponsor

assumes vicariously the duties of religious motherhood that belong to the Church.

Again, however, in this seemingly neglected position, the glorious outlines of the mother come forth the more distinctly. As the Church exalted the natural maternal instinct, so here also she gives the religious accent to the mother's natural selflessness. With the offering of the child to God, the mother's destiny in its deepest sense is also given to God. The mother of the baptized child is the mother as daughter of the Church. Like her own child, she too was once presented by her mother to God. Together, as bound by the most profound union of destinies, the Church and the mother intone the *Magnificat*, that triumphal song of the mercy that is "from generation to generation".

The second birth of the child is concluded in its religious education. The woman, who as mother stands for a part of nature, represents as a Christian mother a portion of the Church. In the religious training of the child, the Church acts through the mother as through one of her members, while the mother functions consciously as a member of the Church. This means that from the mother of the baptized child a light falls once more upon nature as the first step toward grace. For the mother the natural process of expecting the child repeats itself as a spiritual process. Again the same stream of life circulates through mother and child, but instead of the shared physical space they have entered a spiritual area; the forces of blood have given place to the powers of the spirit.

Again the woman is expectant. The character of this expectancy implies that the child which she is awaiting is not actually formed by her, but from her. At the moment of conception she did not take it, but received it; therefore she could not consciously fashion it according to her wishes.

She could carry only that which was confided to her, placing her strength at the disposal of the child, while allowing this strength to be used. That which held good in the physical development of the child is true also of its spiritual growth. The attitude of the Christian mother remains that of the expectant one. In bringing up her child she cannot fashion it according to her own wishes; she can only foster and protect that which was entrusted to her. This, in its religious sense, means the divine image in the growing human being. The child that in the natural sense the mother conceived by its father is in the religious sense the child of the Creator. He creates; she cooperates, with reverence. If the character of nature as the preliminary condition of grace revealed itself in the physical mother, when regarding her as the Christian mother it becomes manifest as the cooperation of the creature with the divine action.

In the light of this fact, the great theme of the Marian dogma refers also to the maternal woman. The cooperating creature is the daughter of the Eternal Woman, the reflected carrier of the Fiat mihi. If the attitude of the Christian mother toward her child is derived from its character as a child of God, her bearing toward her own maternal destiny is inspired by the life of Mary.

The Christian interpretation of the life of a mother builds itself up in three steps, corresponding to the threefold form of the Rosary in its joyful, sorrowful, and glorious mysteries. As this great, popular, and at the same time highly contemplative prayer represents praying to Mary as Mother, so it likewise betokens the proper prayer of the mother. It is the chain of pearls that links the life of the Christian mother to that of the Eternal Mother. Into this threefold prayer the praying woman includes the mysteries of her own motherhood, that through the mystery of the Mother of all mothers they may be uplifted. The earthly mother also has received her child from God; as his gift she has carried it and given it birth. Like Mary, she has presented it to God in the temple, and like her she has found it again in the temple.

While the joyful mysteries contemplate the life proper to the Mother, the sorrowful mysteries consider only the life of the Son. They make no mention of the Mother, for she lives in her Child; his sufferings are enclosed within her life as the sorrowful mysteries are included in the *Ave Maria*. As the mother could not of her own power form either the body or the soul of her child, so she is likewise unable to determine its destiny. The child comes into life; she but cherishes it, which means that sooner or later it will progress beyond the mother. It must advance beyond her. As every life is independent as an existence, so also it is independent as a mission.

The mother lives in the child, but the child does not live in the mother. Every mother's destiny is, in the last analysis, the unending renewal of the pangs of giving birth. To give life to a child means fundamentally that the child detaches itself from her life. In the anguish of birth only the first stage of this process accomplishes itself. For every mother, sooner or later the hour comes when she, like Mary, must seek her child, sorrowing; another, a heavier hour comes when the child may say: "What have I to do with you?" The Island of Riches of which Ruth Schaumann writes in her book *Yves*, by which she designates that blessed solitude of mother and child, usually becomes for the mother at a certain time of her life an island of painful loneliness. There is no loneliness on earth like that of a mother; she is not being parted from some other loved one, but the sword that pierces her heart separates her from her own flesh and blood.

Sooner or later, concealed or unconcealed, the image of the Sorrowful Mother, the Pietà, appears over the life of every mother. In the book of destiny the names of the sorrows of mothers are manifold. They include the suffering over the child that by a necessity of nature must go its own way, down to the estrangement between the generations, even to the complete loss of the child through misfortune, guilt, or death. Under the religious aspect all these griefs of the mother have but one name, the name by which Sigrid Undset entitled the third volume of her great novel. It is *The Cross.* Kristin Lavransdatter, who sacrificed for her children even her relationship to a loved husband, ends in complete estrangement from her older children. Her youngest and dearest child dies, while she herself dies for a strange child. With this conclusion the whole way of the sorrowful mother is traversed.

The rending of a child from its mother fulfills itself most radically through death, by which the Cross rises in its most unmistakable form, in the presence of a mother's love. It is in the death of the child, however, that the detachment of the child from its mother appears in its true religious significance. Like a falling light this meaning plunges from the fact of death through all the forms of maternal tragedy. As Mary's sorrow was fundamentally determined through the work of redemption on the part of her divine Son, so the most profound interpretation of every maternal sorrow is associated with the designation of the child for God. The Son who was presented in the Temple is basically already the One who died on the Cross, but he who died on the Cross remains also the One who was found in the Temple. As the second to the last decade of the joyful mysteries points toward the sorrowful mysteries, so likewise the last decade of the sorrowful Rosary swings back as it were into the joyful, and beyond it. The glorious mysteries mean transfiguration. The Son, ascended into heaven, draws his Mother after him. The unloosing of the child from its mother, understood in its ultimate religious significance as the destination of the child for God, concludes in God, the final, the indissoluble union.

This union is twofold. The ascended Christ, who drew his Mother into heaven to be with him, is also the Christ who continues to dwell upon earth, and Mary's life of glory companions her life in the Church. With the words from the Cross, "Behold thy Mother, behold thy son", the dying Saviour summons the disciple to be Mary's spiritual son, and Mary to be the spiritual mother of the disciple. St. John stands for the Apostles in general, and all those whom the disciples of the Lord baptize for Christ are also the children of Mary. In that hour when her life as Mother of Christ seems fully concluded, she becomes in truth the universal Mother of Christians.

For the second time the words of the *Magnificat* are fulfilled: "And all generations shall call me blessed!" The Gospel does not speak of Mary again, but the Acts of the Apostles show her to us, much as the great religious art of the Christian West has painted her: with the Apostles in Jerusalem, awaiting the coming of the Holy Spirit. As the words of the *Magnificat* fulfilled themselves a second time in Mary when she stood beneath the Cross, so on the morning of Pentecost for the second time the Holy Spirit descends upon her, and the Mother of Christ becomes the great Mother figure of Christ's Church.

For the individual woman as a daughter of Mary, this means that in the Church, by reason of her religious mission, her apostolate as mother, the woman has her place beside the bearer of religious fatherhood, beside the priesthood of the man. Only in this apostolate are Christ's words

"Whoever receives one such little child in my name receiveth me" fulfilled for the woman, not only in their supreme, but also in their actual sense. The life of the Church as religious life is the life of Christ growing within the human soul. As the global form of the earth, uplifted into a sacred symbol, appears in the cupola of a cathedral, so at this point the religious concept assumes the primal form in order to elevate it. We have seen the compassionate love of the maternal woman extend itself into a universal motherliness, through the need of her own child for care and protection. We see this universal motherhood uplifted by religious vocation into the service of the growing Christ within the souls of men. The ray from the crown of the Mother of Mercy parallels the radiance from the crown of the Mother of Divine Grace.

The woman as mother was not made the subject of a special act of consecration, nor does her apostolate receive this distinction. It is but a part of the Lay Apostolate in which every Christian may participate. The mother never fulfills herself in the mother, but in the child. The Great Sacrament rests upon the Son of the Mother, not upon the Mother herself, but by this very fact the mission of woman in the Church touches closely the essential quality of the Church herself. In her character as mother, the Church is a cooperating principle; the One who works within her is Christ himself.

Here lies the most fundamental reason why it was fitting that the priesthood was never entrusted to the woman. It is the same reason that determined St. Paul to require that the woman be veiled when attending religious service. The priesthood could not be confided to woman, for thereby the very meaning of woman in the Church would have been annihilated. A part of the essential nature of the Church of which woman is the symbol would likewise have been annihilated. St. Paul's request does not indeed represent a custom dependent upon temporal conditions, but it portrays the demands of the supratemporal Church upon woman who, in her religious significance, is timeless woman.

Like natural birth, religious birth is profoundly concealed. The Church also can say of herself what God disclosed to Moses, namely, that he would allow all his glory to pass over him and let him preach the Name of the Lord; that to whomever he is gracious, he is gracious; that upon whomever he has mercy, he has mercy; but that no one may look upon his countenance. The essentially spiritual life of the Church is hidden; hence, the inevitable error of judgment in those who venture to pronounce upon and even criticize the religious life of the Church from without. This is an absurdity comparable only to that of demanding of the surgeon that his dissecting knife locate the soul within the body.

We have said that woman, by her apostolate as mother, comes into most intimate relationship with the inner life of the Church. She does this by means of her own hidden nature, for in the Church the apostolate of woman is first of all one of silence, and it is in the central enclosure of the sacred place that the religious character of woman necessarily carries its strongest emphasis. The apostolate of silence means that woman is called upon above all to represent the hidden life of Christ in the Church. Therefore, as the bearer of this religious mission, she is the daughter of Mary.

This intimates the maternal apostolate of woman in its ultimate depth. Only a time like that of the recent past, which often has failed both in a religious and in a natural sense, could conclude from this apostolate that it meant underrating woman. One could never dare to combat this error with the feeble assurance that here and there woman had labored and spoken within the Church, for she has never done so within the sacred precincts of the priesthood. The direct charismatic vocation, which in individual cases as in that of St. Catherine of Siena has broken woman's silence in the Church, fulfills itself only in extraordinary situations. It is never according to the usual order of things, and here this order means that, also in the life of the Church, the sources of things lie in hidden places.

In relation to this thought, we come upon an extraordinary piece of writing. In *The Tidings Brought to Mary*, Paul Claudel, with a depth that is almost terrifying, portrays the significance of woman in the Church. His writings differ from all other contemporary poetry and dramatic art, in fact from nearly all the writings of the past few centuries, not only as a result of the determining influence of generally Christian and religious thinking, but because it is permeated with the concept of dogma. In this lies the unique sublimity that is characteristic of Paul Claudel; this too is the cause of his extreme loneliness.

Under the symbol of the awakening of Mara's dead child through Violaine, the leper, *The Tidings Brought to Mary* portrays the birth of life as coming from the utmost depths of the religious principle. Violaine, the broken vessel of the sacrifice, is made worthy of this birth after having offered to God the surrender of her entire life and accepted the terrible illness that means complete expulsion from human companionship. According to Claudel, the man is the active power in the Church. "O God, I thank You for having created me a father of churches", says the architect, Pierre de Craon. "Man is the priest; but woman's gift is to sacrifice herself." The mystery of religious motherhood touches the priestly mystery of the Consecration through Violaine's miracle, which remains hidden yet transforms everything. The dark eyes of the awakened child become luminous like the eyes of Violaine before her illness, but Mara, the defiant, the selfish one, from whom the child inherited her black eyes, finds forgiveness and solace at last in that she may be a sister to Violaine. Souls are transformed. Violaine's miracle happens in the blessed night of Christmas.

Always and everywhere, contact with the Church means participation in her universality. Beneath the Cross where Mary was proclaimed the spiritual Mother of all Christians stands not only the woman who has offered her own child to God, but also the woman who has sacrificed to God the wish or the hope for a child of her own, or who was willing to give a child to God. The mother of Christ growing within the soul is the mother who folds the hands of her child in prayer; it is also the nun who lovingly gives support to her spiritual daughters on the heights of the religious life. It is Monica, the great saint of mothers, who by her prayers gave life to her son a second time and changed Augustine into Saint Augustine. It is also the virginal saint, Catherine of Siena, as *dolcissima mamma*, "sweetest mother", to her spiritual son. It is the lonely woman upon her sickbed who can but carry the growing Christ within her own soul.

Contact with the Church, as we indicated above, always implies a certain universality. Hence, in the religious sphere, the mother becomes the all-inclusive form of woman's life, in fact the absolute form. This absolute position into which the Church places the mother means that the all-embracing form of motherhood, because it is all-embracing, must include also the virgin. Upon the summit of the religious mission of woman, the conclusion swings back to the beginning. Over the timeless woman the image of the Eternal Woman appears. The religious mother concept of the Church is indissolubly bound to her who as Virgin is Mother and as Mother is Virgin.

Here the tremendous meaning of the dogma for every individual woman's life unfolds once more. The all-embracing form implies also the all-encompassing task. For the woman who prays, the contemplative prayer of the Rosary represents her own life as affiliated with the life of Mary. The Rosary, as the great mother prayer to a Mother, introduces every separate maternal mystery of Mary with the invocation of the Virgin; but every such invocation is followed by the contemplation of a mystery of motherhood.

Upon the interpenetration of these two mysteries when expressed in the sorrowful Rosary rests the unutterable impression of Michelangelo's Pietà. In the startling youthfulness of Mary, who in final agony renders her dead Son back to God, the gentle Virgin of the Fiat mihi—"Be it done unto me"—appears again. When the mysteries of the Virgin and the Mother unite in the joyful decades, they find their image represented in Tiepolo's painting of St. Rose of Lima, to whom the Madonna is giving the Christ Child.

From this point a final inclusive view of the Christian woman becomes possible. She is not simply the Christian woman; she is woman placed in an order of life ordained by God. Every stage of this life denotes a complete and an independent fulfillment, but also a bond of union with the collective and primal image of woman's life. The life of every woman is immediately concerned with the unfolding of this image, be it a partial representation as virgin or mother. But at the last it is a matter of the reconstruction of the eternal image. The virgin must accept the idea of spiritual motherhood, while the mother must repeatedly return to a spiritual virginity. Upon the success of this interchange the well-being of every woman depends, as also does the victory over what may be the tragedy of the unmarried woman or that of the mother.

This means nothing other than that the salvation of every individual woman is indissolubly bound not only to the image of Mary, but also to Mary's mission. The conscious reproduction of the eternal image is possible for the individual woman only in the attitude of handmaid of the Lord, in the constant readiness of her surrender to God. The involuntary confirmation of this absolute meaning and requirement on the part of the eternal image, however, extends far down into the secular world. Even aside from a woman's Christian obligation, the balance proper to her life, the overcoming of its tragic elements whether in the unmarried or the maternal state, can be accomplished only through an approach, albeit unconscious, toward the reproduction of the eternal image.

Mary does not signify only the salvation of the woman, but also salvation through the woman. If it is the individual woman's concern to reproduce this eternal image in her life, its restoration must be of import likewise for the world. Violaine's sickness, in Claudel's story, stands in relationship to original sin. "O Violaine, O woman, through whom the temptation came!" Pierre de Craon cries out, but this illness is also related to the special sin of the times. The book is permeated with the apocalyptic atmosphere of our own day, but mirrored in the closing medieval period which in its chaotic disorder approached but did not equal our times.

The rebirth of the dead child transforms the souls of those concerned and, through them, also the world. When, on the same Christmas night during which Violaine's miracle takes place, a renewal in the worldly order begins, it is but the reflection of this inner transformation. The king, who puts an end to the state of confusion in his country, is led to coronation by St. Joan, Violaine's spiritual sister. The birth from out of the depth of religious life is, at the final issue, the new birth of life itself. For this reason, in Christian countries, our ancestors placed Mary's image not only over the entrance to their churches, but also over the doors of their homes, their town halls, and their market place.

What Pierre de Craon says of the martyr Justitia is as true of Violaine as it is of St. Joan: "She too was only a modest little girl until God summoned her to the avowal of her vocation." As they both came out of obscurity, so into obscurity they returned. Violaine opens the way for Pierre de Craon. He strides out into the world of great undertakings, while she disappears under the veil of the leper, as St. Joan does under that of the funeral pyre. Pierre, the "father of Churches", builds the cathedral whose mighty vaults "rest on the cornerstone of Justitia's tender remains". Joan's work, however, is completed by the men of her people. She too but opened the way for them. The salvation that woman brings ranges far beyond her; its proper fulfillment, its success upon earth, is man's appointed mission.

And now the last of the three great forms of woman's life reappears, that while it reflects, it may also become part of the eternal image. Mary as Virgin Mother is likewise the spouse of the Holy Spirit. Again the great paths of woman's life intersect. Violaine, who as a virgin represents the image of the mother, stands at the same time upon the double line of the Christian spouse. It is the child of the man whom she loves and who at one time was destined to be her husband that she restores to life, but she does it as the spouse of Christ.

As the renewal of culture depends on whether the other half of reality, the woman's countenance, becomes visible again in the face of the creative man, so the true salvation of the world depends on whether Mary's features grow visible also in his face. The announcement made to Mary is fundamentally an annunciation to the whole human race. The bride who in the eyes of man represents the virgin and the mother represents also the Virgin Mother; she represents, in fact, the Marian influence in the life and work of man, and she does it as the half part of his own reality.

We have come to the ultimate consideration. Woman's mission, winging far beyond the woman herself, touches the mystery of the world. The Annunciation to Mary is a message to every creature, but to the creature as represented in Mary. The renewal of the eternal image through the Marian mission of the woman completes itself in the vicarious role of her who represents the creature. Mary stands for her daughters, but her daughters must also stand for her. In Claudel's poetry the apocalyptic line curves into the atmosphere of Advent. It is Advent until the coming of Christ on Judgment Day! But again, as always, the Annunciation to Mary precedes the fulfillment through Christ, vision follows upon concealment, as redemption does upon the humility of acquiescence, as the unfolding of heaven upon its willing acceptance, upon the Yes of the creature.